xo
Olive —
You are Remarkable !
Karlee

NOW
BOARDING

NOW BOARDING

Next Stop–Your Remarkable Life

Kandee G

Now Boarding: Next Stop—Your Remarkable Life

© 2005 Kandee G

Manufactured in the United States of America.

For information, please contact:
Brown Books Publishing Group
16200 North Dallas Parkway, Suite 170
Dallas, Texas 75248
www.brownbooks.com
972-381-0009
A New Era in Publishing™

ISBN 1-933285-14-1
LCCN 2005929900
1 2 3 4 5 6 7 8 9 10

Dedication

I dedicate this book to all that is real: to love and truth. And in that I say to my sweet daughter Katie, you gave me the courage and the strength to put one foot in front of the other; I love you so much. To my beloved Dave, you are proof that real love exists; you have my heart. And to Kelly and Erin, you are such an important part of this journey, my love to you. My love to all of you.

Contents

Acknowledgments

There are so many who have have contributed to the dream of formalizing real tools to make a real difference. To each of you who has and continues to play a part in this dream, I thank you with all my heart.

In particular, I would like to acknowledge: Christine Richard, Jacqueline LaScala, Catrina Roesch, Simone Labrador, Krista Kersey, Robin Aston, Sandy Rathbun, Ellis Jackson, Anne Goldberg, Rachel Nash, Ali Garcia, and the entire team of remarkable people at Kandee G Enterprises, Inc., whose vision and sense of purpose are unparalleled.

To the incredible creative team at Brown Books, especially Kathryn Grant, Milli Brown, Rhonda Porterfield, Erica Jennings, and Deanne Dice: thank you, thank you.

To Les Brown, my great friend and mentor, my gratitude is deep and abiding.

Thank you to all of you who have attended my lectures, seminars, and coaching sessions; having you cross my path has meant more than I can express on this page.

And mostly, thank you to my family: Katie and Dave. Your support, your wisdom, your encouragement, and your love mean everything.

Foreword

A remarkable life is available to all of us, and Kandee G, internationally recognized speaker, life coach, and author, gives us the keys to "release the imprisoned splendor" (Elizabeth Browning). The question persists: if it's possible that all of us can live a remarkable life, then why don't we? I have come to believe that the reason some people don't pursue better lives is that they can't see what they don't know, and they don't know what they can't see. Kandee G walks us through the process to realize the things about us that we don't see for ourselves. It's hard to see the picture from inside the frame, so Kandee G provides a mirror.

Once we're on board a plane, the first instruction given is "fasten your seatbelts for safety in the event of turbulence before we reach a comfortable cruising altitude." Most people give up the flight before they ever reach cruising altitude. The turbulence sets in, and they believe they are not going to be able to make it through. The ups and downs, the bumps and air pockets send them back to the ground, and more times than not, they believe the ground is where they belong.

Kandee G's coaching provides guidance and self-management, and has empowered thousands to navigate through the turbulent storms of life. She pulls from her own hardships, setbacks, and challenging experiences as a single mother who went from subsisting on peanut butter to being transported by private jets. Kandee G provides insights and strategies that will give you major breakthroughs in every aspect of your life.

Her principles will teach you how to create a remarkable life. Kandee G is the message that she brings. I've seen her incorporate her message in the raising of her lovely daughter Katie—my "cookie fairy" who is destined for greatness—as well as in the love and support of her husband Dave, the quiet power behind the woman. She has a strong sense of purpose to change the planet and transform people's lives. She lives with passion and is a powerful force to be reckoned with.

Kandee G and I have shared the stage throughout the United States and all the way to London. Everyone has been amazed with the strategic thinking and winning approach they have gained, not only from her speeches and seminars, but also from her celebrated life-coaching program, G.A.M.E.S., A Pathway to Personal Action. *Now Boarding* brings forth a great deal from that program, tied in with Kandee G's own life experiences, and is guaranteed to change your life. This book will enable you to live the life others only dream about.

—Les Brown
Author, *Live Your Dreams* and *Up Thoughts for Down Times*

Letter from the Author

Dear Friend,

Life is here to be completely enjoyed and fully lived. The era of your life that consisted of stark endurance ended when you picked up this book. You have already taken the first in a series of action steps that can ignite your spirit and enliven your existence. As you read the pages that follow, I will share the secret Laws of Life with you. Then I will guide you through G.A.M.E.S., my practical program for making the Laws of Life work specifically for YOU.

Just to get you started, here's the first and mightiest Law of Life: your thoughts are things. They are things that lay out, construct, and dictate your life. I will teach you how to reengineer your thoughts so that you can redesign your life, consciously and deliberately.

I am living proof that the way we think about ourselves, about others, and about our surroundings and our passions drives our lives. Our habitual thoughts and our attitudes literally make our lives take form. Once I truly understood what creative thought was, what it meant, and how, by changing my thought process, I could change everything, I did. That's right—I propelled myself from an existence of meager subsistence to a life of bounty and joy. The steps are simple, but not always easy. If you are willing to do the work, marvelous excitement awaits you. Follow the exercises I provide and you will unlock the tools within yourself for your own fulfillment.

Are you ready? I'll be right there by your side.

Join me on this adventure of possibility!

With love,
Kandee G

Introduction

The Comeback Kid

Do you know what a wellspring is? A wellspring is a source of continual supply. Wouldn't it be delightful if you had a wellspring of energy, of confidence, of optimism, of joy? Wouldn't it be phenomenal if you had a generator powerful enough to supply you with whatever you wanted? And what if this device was always nearby, wherever you went, and you never had to pack it or transport it because it just naturally followed you everywhere?

Well, here's a newsflash: you do have access to this abundance, because you are that wellspring.

All these wonders are locked inside of you. You don't believe me? It takes effort to become aware of our staggering and limitless abilities. Life is work. However, if you have the will to win, you have achieved half of your success. If you do not, you have achieved half of your dissatisfaction and disappointment. This book will help you find whether or not you already have that will and, if you do, it will show you ways to cultivate it and expand it. If you find that life up to now has drained the will to win out of you, then you will learn how to tap your inner resolve and experience drive and vigor once again. Through specific principles and exercises, I will give you the tools to create the extraordinary and magical life to which you are entitled. I want to motivate you to reach new heights, and I will give you the implements to soar higher than you ever dreamed possible.

Right now, you are probably thinking, "Easy for her to say. She has it all: a lucrative profession she loves, a loving home life, all the material things one could ask for." I want you to understand that I created the life I have now from nothing. That's right. I created it. Let me tell you my story.

I was not a planned pregnancy. Born out of wedlock, I became what I call a "throwaway child." I was turned over to relatives who grudgingly took on the unwanted obligation. Grandparents and aunts and uncles shuffled me around the country. I remember becoming aware at about the age of five that I had no father figure, and this missing piece of my identity perplexed me.

Even at a young age, I had a strong faith. One of my early homes was located next door to a Methodist church, and it backed up to acres and acres of deep woods. Both the church and the woods drew me in. After one of my relatives took me to Sunday school, I continued to go, even when no one else in my family did. I would dress for Sunday school, head for the church, and walk up the big stairs alone. There was comfort there. Likewise, I felt solace in the outdoors and spent hours hiking, climbing trees, and communing with nature.

Eventually, I left the country setting and moved to Pittsburgh. It was at this point in my young adult life that I found out the name of my father. I located the house where he supposedly lived and drove to it. But in spite of all the years that I had struggled with the issue of not having a father, I drove away without trying to see him.

As soon as I had graduated from high school and my relatives could rid themselves of the burden of me, they did. I remember the experience as if it were yesterday. Before my eighteenth birthday, I was standing in the driveway, ready to leave, and I was told, "I'm glad you're leaving. Go find a place and stay there. This was never your home." That is how I started my adult life.

As I stood there outside my relatives' home in Pittsburgh, hearing that I was being sent out into the world, I contemplated the things I wanted out of life: happiness, love, financial freedom, knowledge, communication . . . many things that I felt would lead to a life of fulfillment. These goals seemed far away, if attainable at all.

I left Pennsylvania and moved to Florida. I said, "I don't need them! I am going to make my own life work." But, what I found instead was a whole lot of heartache. I will tell you that I made poor choices, and those choices led me into a dangerous period of my life. I was hardly more than a child, working and living without the moral support of a family, and I began to associate with people who, to say the least, did not offer me the smooth transition to adulthood that we all deserve. For a period of about five years, I allowed the circle of people around me to influence my behavior. I abandoned certain values that I had previously lived by. Then, one day, I picked up the newspaper and saw to my shock that many of my "friends" had been arrested. I remember the revelation that dawned on me as I looked at that article. I said to myself, "This is not what God wants me to do." Right then and there, I packed my bags and I walked out the door.

I spent time pondering the immensity of our creation, our physical birth, and our arrival in this world. Surely, I thought, we can't go through such a process just to endure a life of hardship. I began to study a variety of different religions. I began to meditate daily and to explore ways to understand what this entity called God truly was. I decided that I would study people who were successful and happy. It was then that I started my journey, a journey I will always continue.

Eventually, I got married, got a job, started a family, and began to develop my career. I was doing what "they" (those around me—society) said to do. If you get married and get a good job, you're supposed to be happy, according to conventional wisdom. I seemed to have achieved a happy ending. Having gone from a position of great uncertainty, and without a sense of place, to obtaining what were supposedly the ultimate goals, I thought that all was well with the world. Guess what? The happy ending ended! Twelve years ago, my circumstances took a drastic change! Everything I had worked so hard for—retirement account, savings account, investment accounts—was abruptly gone. And I was alone, taking care of my four-month-old baby!

I remember the exact moment that the enormity of my situation struck me. One night, while my baby was sleeping, I walked to the refrigerator and opened the door. I was horrified to see that one jar of peanut butter was the only thing left! I had no family to fall back on, and no money to pay my mortgage. The stress was almost overwhelming. Almost.

I decided then and there that I was not going to be a victim; I would be the victor! Many people sit back and moan about mistreatment. They use others' unfairness as an excuse to give up. I was not going to do that! I decided to reassess my role in life.

I became determined to figure out exactly what I was supposed to be doing and how I would make it work. My personal study of spirituality and philosophy had gone on for close to fifteen years at this point. I had run through mainstream religions, alternative religions, effectiveness gurus like Steven R. Covey, and motivational teachers such as Les Brown (who has since become one of my mentors). In these diverse teachings, I found common threads or truths that would help me on my path. One of the most significant and inspiring themes that I had encountered was this: God has something planned for each of us. Thus, I must not have been "unplanned" after all. I was a planned pregnancy in a much higher sense—one that went well beyond my earthly family. My goal was to discover that plan and put it into action!

From struggling on my own with a four-month-old child to care for, one jar of peanut butter in the fridge, and no money, I have done a few things. I built a sales organization and was recognized as being among the top in my industry. I am now financially independent. I have been interviewed by major publications, television, and radio for my success. I travel nationally and internationally with my mentor, coach, and grand friend, Les Brown. I have flown engine, and engineless, airplanes. I take four to five vacations a year and often travel by private jet. I have never missed one of my daughter's events at school. The finest man I have ever met now walks at my side as my beloved, my best friend, my spiritual partner, a co-parent, and the ultimate playmate. I don't tell you these things to impress you, but to impress upon you that I firmly believe you, too, can have everything you want in this life. I proved that it can be done. I am living it every day!

All of my prosperity, my career, and my plenitude originated in two decisions: first, to see myself as the victor, not the victim; and second, to discover my purpose. Yes, it is possible to discover your purpose. We all have one. And you can uncover what you were truly designed to do. You can release your past; you can reinvent yourself and re-create your own reality. If you apply yourself to understanding the principles, and practicing the activities that I present in this book, you can harness your own powers of creative genius and empower yourself to achieve spectacular results—results even beyond your current dreams.

In the first part of this book, I will explain four Laws of Life—timeless, universal principles that underlie all your future achievements. As significant as these principles are, they are rarely taught or even brought to our attention. And yet reality is bound by these laws, just as surely as it is bound by the principles of math and chemistry and physics that you may have learned in school. Learning these elementary but powerful Laws of Life will give you a sturdy handle on success and will serve as the blueprint for the program described in the second part of the book. These first four Laws will also help you to understand a fifth, all-encompassing Law of Life, described in chapter 7.

At the end of each chapter, I will give you specific exercises to perform. Your participation in these exercises is crucial. Take your time and perform each one, for the journey we are about to take is for you, about you, and within you. Don't shortchange yourself.

In the second section of the book, I will take you step-by-step through my innovative program, G.A.M.E.S., A Pathway to Personal Action. G.A.M.E.S. is a simple but highly effective system I have developed over twenty-five years of study. It will give you well-defined tools that you will be able to use for the rest of your life.

The final section of the book provides two lists intended for quick reference. The first, Appendix A, defines the Laws of Life, and offers brief explanations. The second, Appendix B, offers forty encouraging reminders to help you maintain your daily practices. I am making a personal commitment to you right now: once the book is ended, I am not going to let you go. We are going to create community so that I can help keep you on the path, on your roadway to you.

Let me be your guide. If the remains of your hopes and dreams are buried like an ancient and forgotten city beneath the strata of time, come with me and I'll help you excavate them. Here's a truth I've found: most people bury not only their precious dreams, but also the very tools they need to uncover them. But there is a glorious solution: if you commit to dig beneath those layers—the years, the frustrations, the resentments, the disappointments, the concessions—you can unearth lavish treasures and begin to thrive again. You already own those riches. Why not come with me and reclaim them?

A Message from Kandee G

My personal commitment to you is always to come from my heart as a source of education; to serve as a pathway to your wellness, your personal truth, and your creation; and to be the inspiration for you to take action.

I do not make claims of being a licensed therapist or psychologist. My work is not intended to replace that of a licensed therapist. I am a consultant and personal coach.

In my role as your personal coach, I offer the following contract. This is not a contract with me, but with yourself. Please read, sign, and date it. In doing so, you will be making a firm commitment with yourself to read this book and explore with me the secrets I have discovered that truly make life work. You will be declaring yourself ready and willing to follow the principles I spell out in these pages, and to begin the work that will bring you the rewarding life you deserve.

Please read, sign, and date:

I, _____ , understand that I am undertaking an intensive, directed journey to my own personal truth. I commit myself to my growth. I commit to reading this book and to applying its principles in my daily life. I will do the work I need to do.

_____

Signature

_____

Date

Chapter 1:
Thoughts Are Things

A re you thinking right now? I bet you answered yes to that. But are you sure you're really thinking, or are you being thought? I'll put that in a statement for you: we think that we think, but most of the time, we are being thought. What does that mean? We have 60,000 to 70,000 thoughts a day. Out of all those thousands of thoughts, 80 to 90 percent are the same thoughts we had yesterday, and most of those, we got from someone else! The time has come for you to be a conscious, free, and deliberate thinker. Every thought counts. Every single thought! Here is my first Law of Life, the Law of Creative Thought: thoughts are things. And what you think is what you get.

You may be wondering, what could possibly be so significant about my thoughts? How could every single thought be influential? The answer to that question lies within the concept of "creative thought."

I want you to consider the possibility that your thoughts have enormous power.

In 1860, Wallace Wattles wrote a book called *Financial Success.* The subtitle was *Harnessing the Power of Creative Thought.* Wattles says, "There is a thinking stuff from which all things are made and which, in its original state, permeates, penetrates, and fills the inner spaces of the universe. A thought in this substance produces the thing that is imaged by the thought. A person can form things in his thought and, by impressing his thought upon formless substance, can cause the thing that he thinks about to be created." Thoughts are things.

You probably readily accept the concept that thoughts are creative in the sense of generating actions that deliver what you have thought about. We frequently think of something we need and then, for example, we go out and purchase it. But what about the nonmaterial things in your life? Could your thoughts create them, too? Have you ever thought about someone that you haven't seen or spoken to in a long while, and then soon, for no apparent reason, that person phones you? I want you to consider the possibility that your thoughts have enormous power—yes, even magical power. See more on that subject in chapter 2.

Earl Nightingale, already well into his forties, discovered a statement, twelve words, upon which he built his entire empire. Those twelve words are, "Human thought has a tendency to transform itself into its material equivalent." Jesus said, "As a man thinketh, so shall he sow." Napoleon Hill wrote a book, *Think and Grow Rich*. The title speaks for itself. Think and grow rich.

In her book, *The Field: The Quest for the Secret Force of the Universe*, Lynne McTaggart, an investigative journalist, has presented some fascinating evidence for a physical mechanism behind the creative power of thought. She explains how quantum physicists discovered a participatory relationship between observer and observed in experimentation with quantum particles. She asserts that investigations have suggested that "the consciousness of the observer brought the observed object into being."

Thoughts are things. It has been said that the nonconscious mind creates at a ratio of six to one. This means that the thoughts beneath the conscious thoughts are helping to create your world. In fact, they are even more influential than the thoughts you are aware of. When you don't know what those underlying thoughts are, you may be saying, "I think I'm taking the right action, but I'm not getting the results I want." Have you ever had that experience?

> **The thoughts beneath the conscious thoughts are helping to create your world.**

We are constantly creating with our thoughts, whether we are ignoring them or paying attention to them, whether they are shouting at us or whispering. Now, the creative, compliant part of our universe does not sift through our thoughts and just pluck out the positive, productive, good ones—the negative, doubtful ones get created as well. Les Brown cites some pertinent statistics on the subject of the biology of the psyche. He quotes one study that concludes that negative statements are sixteen times more powerful than positive ones. What exactly does this mean? It means that when you hear a negative statement, you need to hear a positive statement sixteen times in order to counteract the effects of the negative one. Our world is filled with negativity. Ask yourself how often you are in a positive thought process. Just what are you thinking?

You truly can design your own destiny. Here's another essential question to ask yourself. Just what are you feeling? It is vital to understand that emotion is just as creative as thought, because our thoughts and emotions are so intimately linked. Our emotions mold our thoughts, and our thoughts likewise shape our emotions. How often are you experiencing positive emotion? How often do you feel good? George Bernard Shaw says that "life isn't measured by the number of breaths we take, but by the moments that take our breath away." How often do you have those moments? Learn to look in on yourself and observe what kinds of thoughts and feelings you allow to occupy your mind. Remember that these internal raw materials build your exterior reality.

You can learn to rewrite and regulate your creative thought process. We will work on ways to dredge up what is going on in your nonconscious mind, and identify those thoughts that are creating what you don't want. Then we will reveal what you do want, and draw a road map to your fulfillment. When you learn to reengineer your thoughts, you can change your life, consciously and deliberately, and build a highway straight to your dreams. You truly can design your own destiny.

Exercise 1:
Time To Begin

Exercise means to train, to implement, or to apply. At the end of each chapter, you will be asked to do one or more exercises, which serve as training for your new life and your new you. These are all practical applications that help you understand and put into practice the principles discussed in this book. The ideas that I am presenting will not work unless you apply them. Your exercise for this section is to pick up a journal or notebook, something that you will feel comfortable writing in for at least the duration of this book.

Chapter 2:
Focus Forward and Find the Real You

Designing your own destiny may sound like a high-minded suggestion. I wouldn't be surprised if you're even thinking it's impossible. Why? Because our society discourages "magical thinking." Let me give you a real-life example.

Recently, I was chatting with a group of people at a social function, and a complaining father caught my ear. This gentleman felt that his son had a real problem. The son had lofty dreams and big ideas about what he wanted his own life to be, ones that diverged sharply from the path his father had taken. This well educated parent did not understand how his son could ignore the simple "rules" that one should follow: go to school, get an education. He wanted his son to be an attorney, like himself, and he anticipated making the son's way easier than his had been. After a lengthy battle, this gentleman had taken his son to a therapist, who had prescribed antidepressants. That is the society we are creating—one that sadly pretends to offer quick fixes to complex issues.

Magical thinking is the place where real creativity is born.

Why would this father automatically assume that his son's dreams were ridiculous? Obviously, the father had enough confidence in the son's abilities to expect him to become an attorney. If the young man could handle such a long and difficult course of study, why couldn't he manage a demanding path of his own choosing? Why couldn't he succeed at his own ambitions? Our society tends to disregard and disrespect unusual dreams and goals, and tries to direct every person into the same ruts.

Don't let our society do that to you. Learn that there can be as much lofty dreaming as you want. Magical thinking is the place where real creativity is born. Don't be blocked by the skewed views of a society that disdains magical thinking and yet accepts the widespread overuse of antidepressants. Magical thinking works, and I am going to share with you the secret that makes it work. I call it the Law of Focus.

Here's how the second Law of Life, the Law of Focus works: decide what you really want, then consciously, consistently keep your focus on whatever that is, and your energies will create it. The principle sounds easy; however, it requires work. I'll discuss the decision part in chapter 3; right now, I'll explain how you can train yourself to focus fully.

Here's the first action step you need to take: place your focus forward. Too often, we place our attention on things of the past, and that paralyzes us from moving forward. How can we break free from the prison of the past? The answer to that question lies in scripting. What is scripting? Scripting is the sum total of the thought patterns, the past perceptions, and the feelings that run our reactions, our decision-making processes, and ultimately, our lives. Often, we don't know what our own scripting is until we take the time to become consciously aware of it. Where does scripting come from? It comes from parents, teachers, peers, television, the movies we watch, the music we listen to, our past experiences, and other people's expectations—all of this is scripting.

I had a fascinating experience when I was at a conference at a college campus. We talked a lot about the students' aspirations and their passions. There was so much energy and excitement in the room. The students had fabulous ideas and wonderful things they wanted to create, but no one was actually working on his or her own dreams. They were working on the plans they thought they were supposed to have. I asked many of the young people what was keeping them from living their dreams, and they all said the same thing: their parents! Instead of making a conscious decision to focus forward in the direction of their own choosing, they allowed others' past expectations to direct them. Trying to live someone else's dream—this is a perfect example of scripting.

> **If you change your scripting, you can change your life.**

Whether we are aware of it or not, there are voices under our voices—silent voices that are part of our subconscious min and that drive our decision-making processes. We will w on ways to uncover what those silent voices are saying to help change them so that you can build the life you By the end of this book, you will have new scripting.

aware of any conversations playing out in your head? Well, that is scripting. I believe that if you change your scripting, you can change your life.

I have proven that new scripting works!

Once you begin to change your scripting, you reveal the false limitations that have blocked your achievements. Then a whole world of impossibilities becomes full of possibilities, and you can set outrageous goals. I will tell you about a wildly outrageous goal that I have, and how it became a goal—by uncovering my own scripting! I love to sing. My family, however, would walk out of the room when I started to sing. I found myself saying all the time, "God blessed me with a voice to speak, but not to sing." One day I caught myself saying those words, and I realized that the more I repeated them, the less singing ability I would have. "God did not bless me with a voice to sing" was the negative script I had written for myself. Since I was scripting myself into not being able to sing, I decided to change my internal conversation. I also believe you can do anything through coaching, so I decided to hire a voice coach. Now I am learning to sing, and at one of my events, I actually sang a song *a cappella!* Did I do it perfectly? No. However, I have learned where my singing voice lives. I am learning how to use my voice as an instrument, and I am learning that my voice has potential. A few months ago, I didn't even think I could carry a tune. I have proven that new scripting works!

A warning for all the parents out there: beware, because you e scripting your children all the time. The good news is that can script your children in a positive way. Here is one of orite stories about my daughter, Katie. When she was ars old, she came to me and said, "Mommy, I have a goal. I want to dance on stage at Jackie Gleason Theatre." I had no idea where this notion came from, because I was never a dancer. I was always interested in horses, and I had bought us a horse because, as a parent, I wanted her to do as I did. I wanted her to ride and show and to share my love of horses— but she wanted to dance. She said, "I want to dance on stage at Jackie Gleason Theatre, and to do that, I have to join Ballet Etudes." She already knew where to go. She auditioned and joined the ballet company. Seven months later, I watched my then-seven-year-old realize a goal. She danced on stage in front of a sold-out crowd of 800 people! And the truly amazing part is, after she had set her own goal and followed through on it, she said, "Mommy, you know what? You can do anything you want to do in this life. All you have to do is think about it and do it." Now THAT is scripting!

So, pay attention to what you tell your children. Instead of saying, "No, you can never become a rocket scientist," say, "Go! Magical thinking! Go on and have it!" Consider all those lofty dreams of the young and remember this quote by Johannes Brahms: "Straightaway, the ideas flow in upon me, directly from God."

> As you start to pay attention to your own scripting, there will be "aha!" moments.

As you start to pay attention to your own scripting, there will be "aha!" moments. "Wow, this is where my scripting is!" You can change your scripting, but first you must become aware of it. I want you to pay particular attention to something I call "Big Voice/Little Voice." What I am referring to is our self-talk. We have two voices going on inside our head at any given time. Most of the time, the Big Voice is the one telling us we cannot do something. "I can't do this. I can't this. I can't sing." It is usually the Little Voice saying, "Yes, I can. I want to."

I want you to be the observer, the silent witness to yourself. Step outside yourself and listen to the dual conversations going on inside your head. Once you become aware of them, an amazing thing happens—you can shift them. All you have to do is place your attention on those inner conversations, and they start to shift. For example, if your Big Voice is saying, "I can't sing," and the Little Voice is saying, "I can sing if I try," then all you have to do is pay attention to the Little Voice. Automatically, it will become louder than the Big Voice. The bigger voice of negativity, the voice telling you what you cannot do, will start to shrink. Pay attention to the voice that serves you best. Now, does the voice of negativity ever completely go away? It has been my experience that every once in a while it will rear its head, but the more you consciously heed the voice that serves you, the quieter that negative voice will be.

When you reengineer your thinking, your life will change.

Can you begin to see how creative thought works and how your life is directed by the inner conversations you have? Can you see now that these internal dialogues may originate in ideas that don't serve your best interest, and yet may have a powerful influence on you? Consider the price you could pay for ignoring this whole process. You may spend your life devoted to past scripting that came from other people's opinions or fears and from your own unfounded self-doubts. Your thoughts create your life. Decide now if you are slave or master to your own internal dialogue. When you reengineer your thinking, your will change.

In order to rewrite your scripting, you must pay attention to the voice behind the voice. You must begin to hear from yourself in order to understand what you want and need at your core, that place where your real feelings reside. When you discover what lies at your center, and you use your energy to fulfill those needs, then you can be assured that magical thinking will indeed lead to magical things happening. When you focus forward, on what you want the remainder of your life to be rather than on what it has been, you find your true self.

Exercise 2:
Listen and Observe

PART 1: Big Voice/Little Voice

Take your journal and write down any internal dialogue that you are aware of right now. Note any comments you hear in your head, and also any responses you find yourself making. Just what are your Big Voice and Little Voice saying to each other? This will be an ongoing exercise because the more consciously aware you are of the possibility of inner dialogue, the more you will hear.

PART 2: The Power of Focus

This exercise will help you understand the power of focus. You will see that when you start to focus on "something," then that "something" shows up for you. Have you ever thought about purchasing a new car, for example a yellow convertible, and then noticed that every car on the road seemed to be a yellow convertible? Right now, make a decision to focus on some particular characteristic about the people or objects around you. Jot it down in your journal. As you go through your daily routine, notice how that characteristic shows up all around you.

Chapter 3:
The Only One
Accountable for You Is You

The richness of your life is in direct proportion to your willingness to be in your own discovery. Well, what does this mean? It means that it takes work. Life is work. Your life is your responsibility and your goals are your responsibility. But I promise you, it is well worth the effort to accept your own accountability and take YOUR life's journey. Here is the third Law of Life, the Law of Responsibility: you are responsible for you. Regardless of the past, and regardless of what others may want for you, you are accountable for your life, your actions, your reactions, and those things that you bring into creation.

You have already felt the clout you wield when you become conscious of your thoughts and when you focus on thoughts that serve you. Now let's examine the boost you'll get when you take responsibility for your decisions.

Life is a series of constant decisions, and yet we are unaware of most of them.

First of all, what is a decision? A decision is a conclusion or judgment reached, or the making up of one's mind. How do you make decisions? Ideally, by taking issues under consideration and coming to a conclusion. Unfortunately, however, many of the decisions we make do not undergo the process of conscious consideration. What will you wear today? Which way will you drive to work? Will you work? What will you eat for breakfast? Will you have breakfast? Life is a series of constant decisions, and yet we are unaware of most of them. Many decisions are "automatic" because they originate from what we have been taught or what we have "always done." Let's look at your own decision-making processes and see how often you make "automatic" decisions. Consider the following different types of decisions.

Decision by default—When you are making a decision by default, you are allowing your circumstances to dictate your outcome. Here is a simple example. You are at a meeting at work, and donuts are served. You know that donuts are high in sugar, carbohydrates, and fat, and that they have very little nutritional value. But you grab one anyway, and start your day with this "breakfast" because that was what "they" served you. That is a decision by default. You have decided to ignore your own health and nutrition. Remember that it is always your choice to decide how you will nourish yourself. If you are not watchful, you can allow yourself to make default decisions unconsciously all day long.

Decision by negotiation—This type of decision usually comes with an attached prayer or prayer-like bargaining. It sounds something like this: "Dear God, I promise I will do such and such next time, if you take care of this for me today." Negotiated decisions aren't true decisions, because they are not backed by solid intentions. They are merely pleas to get by the difficulty of the moment. The determination necessary for a true change of behavior is usually lacking.

Decision by victimization—This type of decision is made by the person in the victim mindset, who expects things not to work out. For example, a friend asks if "the victim" wants to attend a concert, and he replies, "I never get the time off work I want, so I know I can't go." As subtle as that sounds, this person has just made the decision not to enjoy a great time out with his friends. His own victim mindset short-circuits his decision-making process.

Decision by peer pressure—You are making a peer pressure decision when you are doing something because someone else wants you to do it. How many times have you made a decision based on what friends and family think are the right things to do? My suggestion is to take a look at the people you

> Your decision-making processes are probably similar to those of the people with whom you associate.

spend the most time with, and see how they make decisions. Do your friends and family make good choices? Your decision-making processes are probably similar to those of the people with whom you associate.

Decision by automation—Automatic decisions can be the most insidious. These are decisions to continue doing things the same way you have always done them, constantly and consistently, without conscious consideration. The person who is in a job going nowhere, who says, "This is what I've always done, so I'll just keep doing it," is making an automatic decision. She has just committed herself to a nonconscious decision that most likely will lead to a life of mediocrity and unhappiness.

Can you see by these examples that you may be making decisions without consciously evaluating situations? And that these unconscious decisions are nonetheless driving your life? You can train yourself to be a decision maker. It is not always easy; as a matter of fact, it can be downright hard, but it is crucial that you utilize the process of conscious consideration. This means looking at an issue, accepting the responsibility to use your own judgment, taking the time to research possibilities, and coming to your own conclusions. It involves making up your own mind, regardless of what anyone else may think or do. When you follow through with this practice, you are really in your own true decision-making process.

You can train yourself to be a decision maker.

There is something very potent about making a decision. When you make decisions consciously and deliberately, then you have set into motion a union of ownership and energy. Settling on something of your own personal choosing with a fixed purpose puts energetic forces into play. Determination and resolution are natural by-products of genuine decision-making. These dynamic forces grant you the conviction to scatter all doubt and leave you ready to face anything to carry out your task or action.

The decision-making process is huge. We have spent time on the mechanism of becoming aware of how and why you make the decisions you do. Now I want to delve into another aspect of decision-making, that of goal-setting. I like to use a template which I call O.W.L. for designing goals; it's a formula for inner wisdom. What does O.W.L. stand for? Obedience. Willingness. Listening. Here's how it works. Let's say that I am formulating a new goal, and I am considering learning to sing. But is this really a goal that suits me? Let me run it through the O.W.L. template to test it.

First, "O" is for Obedience. To thine own self be true. Is this really what I want to do? Does learning to sing comply and conform with me and my desires? In my case, yes. Ask yourself if the goal you're considering is a good fit for you.

> Ask yourself if the goal you're considering is a good fit for you.

Next, "W" is for Willingness. Do I have the willingness to do the work it takes to get there? Yes, absolutely! I want to sing well and I am willing to commit the time and effort it will take. Ask yourself if you have the willingness to do whatever it takes to create your own goal, to arrange your life in such a way that this dream becomes a reality.

And last, "L" is for Listening. Listening to your own thoughts, your own truth, the wisdom of your own heart. We all have this incredible internal wisdom that tells us what to do, that talks to us. It is a small, still voice inside telling us whether or not this is the direction to go. Ask yourself, "Is this something I really want to do, or am I doing it for other reasons?" In my case, yes, I want to learn to sing, because I love the emotion I feel when I am singing.

You can use the wisdom of O.W.L. to examine goals in many different areas of your life, such as mental goals, health goals, emotional goals, and financial goals, as well as career, family, social, relationship, spiritual, and play goals and—one of my personal favorites—wildly outrageous goals. Use the list of categories at the end of this chapter to help generate potential goals. Run each of them through the O.W.L. template. By doing so, you will be able to discover whether a particular goal is compatible with you, whether you want it badly enough to work for it, and whether the desire for it originates within you or in something outside yourself.

While you are considering your decisions and evaluating your goals, I want you to know that it really is possible to discover your purpose, to release your past, to reinvent yourself, to rewrite your story, and it is possible to turn personal mayhem into magic. I am living proof that whatever you want to unfold in your life is truly possible.

Set a goal ... and you can make it happen.

Remember: it's not that people aim too high and miss; they aim too low and hit. Have you made a hit? I truly believe in wildly outrageous goals. The bigger and wilder and grander I create them, the more I realize that I really can have anything I want in my life. You have the ability to do or create whatever you want, if you have that small, still voice inside talking about it. Look deep within yourself and find something you really want to do, something you never thought you could. Last summer, I soared over the top of Mount Shasta, a snow-capped mountain peak over 14,000 feet high—in a plane with no engine! Do you think that is a wildly outrageous goal? Set a goal, no matter how outrageous, and you can make it happen.

When you make your own decisions, you are in charge of your life. The most significant question to ask yourself in this regard is, "Who is in charge of my decisions?" The answer to this question is electrifying. Recharge yourself with it!

Exercise 3:
O.W.L. Formula for
Inner Understanding

O	W	L
Obedience	Willingness	Listening

List some of your goals, using O.W.L.

Mental:_____

_____

Health: _____

_____

Emotional: _____

_____

Financial:_____

_____

_____

Career:_____

_____

_____

Family:_____

_____

_____

Social: _____

_____

_____

Relationship:_____

_____

_____

Spiritual: _____

_____

_____

Play: _____

_____

_____

Wildly outrageous: _____

_____

_____

Chapter 4:
You Don't Have To Know the How, Only the What

I am the most ordinary person I know. I am ordinary, and yet I am living an extraordinary life. Why? Because I made this decision: never give up and never give in. Sorrow plays a role in every life, but here is a bright truth for you to hold always in your heart: our birthright is prosperity and abundance and happiness and joy. If you use this certainty as your foundation, you can build your life in the most remarkable way. And here's some more good news: the fact that you have read this far means that you have already begun the journey you are meant to take in this life—a journey of bounty.

My message to you is this: it is possible. What do I mean by "it"? Your "it" is your unique purpose, that special thing that inspires you to action. Take the time to spend with yourself, and uncover your goals and your dreams. In doing that, you are going to discover your "it." We all have a purpose, something that enlivens and enriches us. Find that special pursuit that infuses you with energy, that thing you want to do more than anything else. What do you want to shoot for? What undertaking engrosses you? What venture entices you? Every person has a purpose, and it is possible to discover yours!

I challenge you to take the information in these pages and put it into action.

I challenge you to take the information in these pages and put it into action. It does not work unless you work it. So, use your newfound decision-making processes and make the decision right now to engage yourself in the action steps ahead.

Did you make that decision? Take this opportunity to look around at your life and find places where you can aim bigger. I want you to open up your mind to greater prospects and aim high. Don't get hung up in the "how." Delete thoughts on how to accomplish these grander enterprises. Pause a moment here and just let your mind expand and explore what you want to do bigger in your life.

Did you free yourself from old boundaries and allow your ambitions to skyrocket? Did you focus on the voice that said, "I want to do this," instead of the voice that said, "You'll never be able to do that"? Did you ignore the inclination to rein in your grand ideas, even though you didn't know HOW to achieve them?

If you had difficulty letting go, refusing to believe that you don't need to contend with the "how" of enacting your dreams, then read on. I'm going to share a Law of Life that may be new to you, even though the wisdom behind it is ancient. This is my fourth Law of Life: the Law of Attraction, and it states this: whether you realize it or not, you are always attracting, into your life, people and situations. Before you read any farther, I want you to reread what the Law of Attraction states, and pause a moment to consider its consequences.

Now, here's how you can use the law: the way to attract things you want into your life is to be what you want to attract. Become it. Become what you want to attract. It takes time and effort, but it pays big dividends. You may hear a voice in your head right now saying, "I can't become those things that I want." Consider the answer Arnold Schwarzenegger once gave when someone asked him what the one key to his success was. He replied, "I never listen to anybody who says I can't do it." You have the option. You have the choice. Create your own belief. By identifying yourself with your desire already fulfilled, you become it. Once you become it, what happens? You kick in the Law of Attraction and you start attracting to yourself those things that you want. Try it. Test it out and see that when you accept this principle and live by it consciously, you create a momentum that becomes self-fulfilling.

I want you to understand that your acceptance and conscious practice of this concept is one of the most important secrets for realizing your **Become what you want to attract.** goals. The Law of Attraction explains why we don't have to be concerned with the details of HOW we will accomplish a cherished goal. But it is crucial to understand that in order to attract desirable things into your life, you need clarity of intent. What I mean by this is that we must clearly establish what our objective is and what our intention is, before the process can work to our benefit. When we can discover our "it," define our right target, and then learn to place our attention on that intention, life will conspire to help us create the things we want. If we can get the self-serving part of the ego completely out of the way, then our intentions will attract the elements, the people, the events, the situations, the circumstances, and the relationships necessary to fulfill that intended outcome.

When acknowledging goals, we do not need to become involved in the details of the how.

What do I mean by the ego? The ego can be defined as the normal, sound part of the psyche that is conscious and that most immediately controls thought and behavior. It can also be an inflated sense of self-importance. In your journey of self-discovery, you must learn to discern the difference between an exaggerated feeling of superiority and an appropriate pride in yourself. The self-involved portion of the ego can mislead you and create a rocky path on the way to your goals. On the other hand, a balanced ego, with a fair sense of self, can help guide you to your heartfelt dreams. So the question becomes, how do we know when we are experiencing out-of-balance ego, or just healthy self-esteem? I find the best way is to ask yourself certain questions when you are struggling with the ego issue. First, evaluate the action you are considering and ask, "Is it true to my sense of fairness, is it necessary, and is it kind?" Next, ask yourself, "Whom does this action serve?" If your action would be dishonest, unnecessary, or unkind, or if it serves only you and not some greater good, then most likely your self-indulgent ego has called you to do it.

I'll repeat this important point: when acknowledging goals, we do not need to become involved in the details of the how. We need only to develop real clarity of intent, free of the unbalanced ego, and hold that intention. We will then start to draw what we want toward us.

I'll give you an example from my life. Recall that I made the decision to learn to sing, even though I had always thought singing was beyond me. Here are some details of that story. Once I chose the path to sing, I was very clear in my intention. And, in accordance with that clarity of intention, an opportunity presented itself at an event I was conducting at a local school. After I had spoken, one of the teachers approached me and told me how much she had enjoyed the program and how much she loved my energy and what I had to say. I asked her what she did, and she said, "I'm the theater teacher here." It was a natural opening for me to ask if she knew a voice coach, since I wanted to learn to sing, and she said, "I teach voice, and I would be happy to teach you to sing." She has been teaching me to sing since that day. You see how easily this marvelous teacher came into my life! Once I became clear on what I wanted, it showed up for me.

When you can unearth what you truly want, magic happens. But there will still be work to do. I can't sing if I don't practice and find the time for my lessons. Remember that the richness of your life is in direct proportion to your willingness to be in your own discovery. Life is work. Your life is your responsibility and your goals are your responsibility.

When you can unearth what you truly want, magic happens.

It can be frightening to set goals beyond the limits you have set for yourself in the past. You can, however, work past the fears and take the risks. The first thing you need to know about facing your fears is what I call "the dream stealers." What are dream stealers? These are the thoughts that keep you out of action. While you spend time with yourself, developing an understanding of your purpose, also take the time to listen to thoughts that steal your dreams. Do you dwell on thoughts of what is lacking in your life, or put energy into wistful longing for something you want as if it's impossible? For instance, "I don't have enough money this week to meet the bills," or "I wish I had a bigger house." These thoughts are creative, too! But they are creating more of what you don't want.

Take the time to listen to thoughts that steal your dreams.

Focusing your thoughts on what you don't have just creates more of what you don't have. Fear creates more fear. Wanting and wishing just creates more wanting and wishing. And trying to live someone else's dream, as I discussed before, is one of the biggest dream stealers of all.

Don't let the dream-stealers rob you. Mold yourself into a dream-maker. Hold within your heart the certainty that you are capable of earning more income, or of learning a new skill, or of achieving more than you have up to now. Don't squander your thoughts and energy pining and yearning. Stay in the vision of what you really want, of what your aspirations are—not those of your family, your friends, or your peers, and not those of society. Staying in the vision of what you really want will help to create it. Do you know what you want? It has been my experience that a lot of people don't.

The truth is that we are creators, and we have the power to consciously create. So what keeps us out of our creative selves? Mostly, it is our limited beliefs. Here is a quote from Marianne Williamson that I want to share with you: "Our deepest fear is not that we are inadequate. Our deepest fear is that we are powerful beyond measure. It is our light, not our darkness, that most frightens us. We ask ourselves, 'Who am I to be brilliant, gorgeous, talented, fabulous?' Actually, who are you not to be? You are a child of God. Your playing small doesn't serve the world. There's nothing enlightened about shrinking so that other people won't feel insecure around you. We are all meant to shine, as children do. We were born to make manifest the glory of God that is within us. It's not just in some of us; it's in everyone. And as we let our own light shine, we subconsciously give other people permission to do the same. As we're liberated from our own fear, our presence automatically liberates others."

How do we recognize limiting beliefs, and how do we change them? The answer to those questions lies in another question: "What are you thinking?" Here is a quote by Jim Rohn that I love: "The

We are all meant to shine.

only limitation that we put on our ability is our inability to easily recognize our unlimited nature. It takes effort to become aware of our staggering and limitless abilities. It takes effort to become enthusiastic over a cause or an occupation. It takes effort to continue trying whenever our results, as well as our friends, tell us to give up. It takes effort to feel right about everything that happens, the joys as well as the sorrows of life. It also takes effort to learn to love ourselves above all others, especially when we are so consciously aware of our failures and our doubts, as well as our tragedies. It doesn't, however, take effort to fail. It requires little else than a slowly deteriorating attitude about our present, our future, and ourselves. It is ironic that one of the few things in life over which we have control is our attitude." And it is our thoughts that control our attitude.

Uncover your dreams.
Nurture your dreams.
Support your dreams.
I'd like to remind you that it was when I had a baby to care for, no money, and only one little jar of peanut butter in the fridge, that I decided I was going to build a sales organization. I decided to do this because I wanted to achieve a certain income level, and I wanted to have the freedom to take care of my daughter in any situation. I actually had someone who was very important to me sit me down, look me straight in the face, and say, "Kandee, what you want to do is impossible." I am living proof that you do find ways to accomplish outrageous goals when you understand your own natural desire and make a conscious decision to aim for it. Just put your foot on that path. It doesn't matter what anybody else says or does. Uncover your dreams. Nurture your dreams. Support your dreams. And don't let others interfere with your dreams.

It is a wonderful feeling to know that the only real limitations you have are the ones you place on yourself. It opens up a world of possibilities. Rumi, the thirteenth-century poet and scholar, says that we search outside for trinkets, while the real treasures are on the inside. I like to take people to their own personal desires through that discovery on the inside. I want to help you find the places where your light shines, and then let it happen!

I am going to make you a promise. There is a special place waiting for you. If you change your scripting, you change your life. You see, you can create your own culture. You don't have to live in anybody else's culture, only your own. You have the power to create it any way you want. As part of the culture that I have created for myself, I make a daily promise to myself and to Katie, and I say this every day: "I promise to drink every dawn like a cup of spring water. I promise to take in every sunset like supper. I promise to make today my best day ever, not to take one breath for granted. I promise to dance every dance like nobody is watching. I promise to love like I will never get hurt. I promise to play until I can't play anymore." This is the culture of Kandee, because this is the way I want to live through this physical incarnation. You can choose to live any way you want. I urge you to be in your own happiness, your passion, your honor, your excitement.

The exercises at the end of this chapter are designed to help you discover your productive and nonproductive conscious and nonconscious thinking. They are also designed to help you uncover your passion and your purpose.

What you do today will shape your tomorrows.

With this information, you can then choose the intentions most worthy of your focus. Once you establish your intent, the next step is to expect those things to happen. Life is a magical place. When you find that inspiring thing, put that call to action. We all have a destiny and a purpose, and sometimes it takes real courage to stay on the path. But remember: what you do today will shape your tomorrows. Stay in your personal development, find your passion, find your purpose, and be in the discovery of you, for it is there that you will find a treasure trove.

Take your time as you work through the questions in EXER-CISE 4. It is important to get your thought processes moving. You may want to choose some relaxing music to play in the background. There is no right or wrong as far as your answers go. The only objective is to unveil you, to give you a pathway to yourself. This is a journey that no one can take but you.

Exercise 4:
Excavate You

PART 1: What Am I Attracting?

Write down what you are attracting into your life right now. What are you attracting that you don't want? Ask yourself what part of you is attracting this situation into your life. Accept personal responsibility for it.

PART 2: What Do I Value?

1. What is my life about? _____
_____
_____

2. What do I value? _____
_____
_____

3. What do I treasure? _____
_____
_____

4. What am I most committed to? _____
_____
_____

5. What do I love? _____
_____

6. What am I most happy about? _____
_____
_____

7. What am I most proud of? _____
_____
_____

8. What am I most excited about? _____
_____
_____

9. What am I most enjoying now? _____
_____
_____

PART 3: Where Is My Greatness Hiding?

1. In my life, currently I wish I had more:_____
_____
_____

2. The greatest thing in my life is:_____
_____
_____

3. My biggest time commitment is: _____
_____
_____

4. When I do the things that I really want, then:_____
_____
_____
_____

5. I feel guilty that I am: _____
_____
_____

6. I worry that: _____
_____
_____

7. If my dreams come true, then: _____
_____
_____

8. I sabotage myself so that: _____
_____
_____

9. I hide my feelings so that: _____
_____
_____

10. I get sad when: _____
_____
_____

Chapter 5:
You Can Reclaim the Path That God Selected for You

L ife can tell you lies. I know this sounds strange, but life is filled with lies, and many of them are perpetrated on you. Here's one of the worst: there is nothing new. You can't create anything new, you can't do anything new, and you can't even imagine anything new. There is only one set of rules, and we all have to follow those same rules to make our lives work. We have probably all been down the road of rules, and for many of us, that course hasn't led to the happiness and fulfillment we expected. And even worse, along the way many of us came to the conclusion that as individuals, we don't really matter. Well, all of that is a lie. It is a lie, a bold-faced lie, no matter who told you, or when they told you—no matter how you got that notion—it is all a lie.

I'd like to share a quote with you that is rich in meaning. This beautiful bit of advice comes from Romans 12:2. It says, "Be not conformed to this world, but be ye transformed by the renewing of your mind, that ye may prove what is good and acceptable and perfect, and that is the will of God." What is this scripture telling us? It is saying that self-renewal is not only possible, but also desirable and healthy! Renewal benefits us and transforms us. Imagine that! We are actually called to find the new, not to ignore it, disregard it, or disbelieve it.

I am going to teach you how to be in the state of constantly renewing your mind.

We can reclaim our excitement.

I have developed a process called reclamation that I will describe in detail in the next section of this book, as I go through the G.A.M.E.S. strategy. For now, I just want you to begin accepting the idea that you can indeed find new avenues in life. You can renew your thought processes. You can rejuvenate that fresh, dazzling sense of possibility that you once had. You can revive old dreams, and you can reclaim the parts of yourself that you have disowned. To disown means to give away. As the years go by, we tend to let disappointments and regrets pile up. We let life's difficulties sap the enthusiasm and vitality we had as children. We disown our zest, our liveliness, our ambitions. But such depletion is not inevitable. We can reclaim our excitement. As you read this book and work through the exercises, you will learn to reclaim your power, your motivation, your joy, your sense of self, and your life.

There are stages to reclamation, and since you have reached this point in the book, you are already in the first stage—the stage of becoming aware that there is something more to life than a daily grind. The next stage of reclamation is seeking to understand. When we read a book or go to a conference, we are seeking to understand specialized knowledge. Once you incorporate enough of that knowledge into your being, it becomes something more elemental than knowledge—it becomes a deep-seated "knowing." That knowing then becomes belief, and we can build belief. When you reach the stage of belief, and you hold to that course no matter what, you awaken to your authentic and true self. You reclaim the essence that you were born with, that spirit and vigor and delight that was meant to be part of you for life.

The next section of this book spells out a systematic program, my G.A.M.E.S. formula, for making your life work for you. The four Laws of Life that you have already learned provide the structure behind this system. In addition, you will learn a fifth Law of Life that is absolutely integral to the reclamation process.

G.A.M.E.S. prescribes certain steps for you to follow each and every day. As you proceed, life will begin to work in a more orderly and desir- **Do you know what rapture is?** able fashion. But understand that it is vitally important to do the work. You cannot guess your way through the process. Every exercise you do will be a part of building toward your reclamation. What is the goal here? The goal is to design a pathway for YOU to have your own personal prosperity. What is personal prosperity? It is abundance in all aspects of your life: health, relationships, success, money, fulfillment, playtime, and love. What is important to you? What do you think will make you personally prosperous?

One of the things that I love to ask people is, "Do you know what rapture is?" Rapture is the state of being carried away with love, joy, and ecstasy. Do you know that rapture is your birthright? You are entitled to rapture. But negativity tends to sidetrack us. As a society, we tend to default to the negative. We let our attention wander and get lost in the maze of naysaying, pessimism, and cynicism.

I want to lead you in your personal search for real feeling, or rapture. This is a journey that you must experience from the inside, and I can assure you that a joyous place does exist there for you. And here is some wonderful news: once you find the path to that place, you can go there anytime! Sometimes I will be grocery shopping, maybe standing in line, and I am just filled with love and joy and ecstasy! It is our birthright! I feel so blessed, and some days I walk around and say, "I must be God's favorite!" But you know what the truth is? We all are. And it is up to us to realize that and to hold that knowledge in our hearts. "I must be God's favorite." I want you to relish that comment for yourself, to feel the comfort and the bliss it bestows when you hear it in your own head.

Rapture is your birthright.

When you can accept that each of us is God's favorite, you are ready to experience miracles. What is a miracle? Look at each letter in the word, MIRACLE, and see that it is a Moment In Right Action, Clearly Leaving Evidence. Once you establish your intention, and begin taking the actions right for you, events will occur that leave evidence of something grander than all of us, something that is helping us to create the things we want in our lives. And miracles happen absolutely every day. Some people might call it a coincidence or happenstance, but once you are awakened to the creative substance of the universe, and to the interaction between your intent and what happens in your life, you will recognize a miracle for what it is: A Moment In Right Action, Clearly Leaving Evidence.

Remember what I said about all of us being planned pregnancies? A power beyond us created you for a reason. You have a purpose, even if you have lived many years without heeding it. You really can reclaim the path that God selected for you.

Are you ready to make miracles happen? Does renewing your mind continuously sound good to you? Do you want to **You have a purpose.** reclaim the vigor you once had? Read on, my friend, The best is yet to be.

Exercise 5:
Recall Your Commitment

Review what you have written in your journal so far, and then reread the contract you signed at the beginning of this book. Consider what is at stake here: Were you satisfied with your life when you began reading these pages? Are you willing to return to the you that first picked up this book? If your answer to these questions is no, then renew your commitment to do the work that will reclaim the happiness and fulfillment you were born to enjoy. It's your dreams that are at stake. Your dreams—your choice.

Chapter 6:
What Simple Strategy Can Make Any Situation Better Instantly?

Y ou are now entering the G.A.M.E.S. zone. Beware: it will change your life. The G.A.M.E.S. formula specifies practical steps to perform every single day. If you do your G, your A, your M, your E, and your S every day, life is going to work for you.

G.A.M.E.S., A Pathway to Personal Action, is the culmination of twenty-five years of personal study, developed from innumerable lectures and personal experiences. As my own life began the process of conscious creation, I knew that one day there would be a way for me to take what I had learned out into the world. I started a company that offers seminars and speaker services. I began to understand that this was my path and ultimate direction. I did not know how it was going to happen, I just knew it was. I stayed in my belief.

Several times in this book, I have used the term "creative substance." I want you to understand this term in reference to something bigger, beyond what we can touch and feel, something that helps create what is going on in our physical lives. Are you open to this possibility? There is a place where thoughts become substance. There is a place from which things become manifest. I want you to accept the existence of this process as part of your reality, and when you do, you will see it at work.

Plato says that a grateful mind is a great mind, which eventually attracts to itself great things. You may say of people who seem to have many blessings that they are so grateful because they have so much. But consider for a moment the possibility that they have so much because they are so grateful. The grateful heart has actually opened to the creative flow, this creative substance, and it becomes the energy that attracts to itself great things. It was because I understood this law of gratitude that the day I stood in my house and looked at that peanut butter jar, I sat down and said my prayers of gratitude. Every day since then, every single day, I look at those things that I am grateful for. My husband Dave says, "I have never seen anybody as grateful as you." For me, it is not just a social grace—it is a part of my being. I live in the consciousness of gratitude.

Live in the consciousness of gratitude.

Gratitude, the first part of the G.A.M.E.S. formula, is represented by the "G." You may be thinking, "Yes, I know I am supposed to be grateful; I know I am supposed to say thank you." But gratitude is far more encompassing than that. We tend to think of gratitude and giving thanks only on the basis of obligation. Our parents taught us as children that when someone does something for us, we are supposed to be polite. It is the rule to be thankful. Although giving thanks is, indeed, an important social grace, inner gratitude is something beyond the niceties of the outside physical world.

Understand this about gratitude: It is not just a reactionary emotion. It is a causative energy. What I mean by this is that gratitude makes something happen. It causes something else. Giving thanks is a state of consciousness that sets the stage for real creating. One can be grateful with the same spontaneity as being happy; it simply comes from within. The best way to use the creative substance is to center yourself in awareness of it, and the best way to do this is to be in the consciousness of gratitude. The grateful heart draws unto itself great things.

The grateful heart draws unto itself great things.

What about the ungrateful heart and mind? What do they attract? An ungrateful perspective, a discouraging and complaining one, will draw unto itself limited things. Many people choose a perspective of inadequacy and insufficiency. What does this create? More limitations! Instead of counting their blessings, they count their envies. Let me tell you what counting your envies sounds like. "She is so pretty." "I wish I had a nice home like they do." Does this sound familiar? The person who wishes or prays for prosperity out of a sense of complaint, discouragement, or envy effectively compounds the problem. There is a subtle difference between aspiring for greater things while acknowledging with gratitude what you now have, and just wishing for more from an ungrateful heart. Take the temperature on your own level of gratitude. Do you perceive a world of "lack and limitation," or a world of abundant, limitless supply? That is a meaningful question to ask yourself.

Feelings are as creative as thoughts.

I once had someone say to me, "Kandee, I am so positive about life, but nothing about life works—it just stinks! I am so positive, but I can't get a job and my car is old, but I am a positive person." Can you see that this person was seriously counting her envies, as opposed to counting her blessings? After we worked together on her perceptions, she came to understand how her own thought processes were holding her back. She put into practice the skills I am presenting in this book. Now she has a forty-hour-a-week job that she loves, and she is creating real income. One of the things this woman learned was that feelings are as creative as thoughts, and the two work together. You may wish for improved financial conditions, but if you are feeling poor, your feeling, the nonconscious state, is what you are projecting and attracting. I would ask you to start giving thanks from the awareness that there is always enough, even if it doesn't seem so.

I love the following story, which illustrates perfectly the difference between the grateful and the ungrateful heart. A missionary in Africa recalled the tale of a mysteriously poverty-stricken tribe. Many of the other local tribes were relatively prosperous. The missionary was curious about this strange phenomenon, and he spent years examining different aspects of the tribe's culture. Eventually, he discovered that they had no word with which to express gratitude. Perhaps it was through some quirk of evolution that they had forgotten how to say thank you. So the question is, could the loss of the spirit of thanksgiving have been responsible for their absence of prosperity?

This example leads us to ask ourselves: could our own financial problems be due to the loss, even temporarily, of our own grateful hearts? There may be someone who would protest and ask, "But how can I be grateful in my situation?"

Whatever your circumstances, I recommend that you stir up the attitude of gratitude. Let me demonstrate why. Read the rest of this paragraph and then do what I describe. Set the book down, close your eyes, and identify something in your life for which you are thankful. Allow gratitude to wash over you. Take your time. Let the spirit of thanksgiving flood your being. Then, when you are deeply into that sense of gratitude, notice your state of mind, how you are feeling.

Pause now and do the exercise. Don't read any further until you have taken a few moments to experience gratitude.

How did you feel once you let gratitude pervade your consciousness? At peace? Joyful? Blessed? Blissful? When you are in gratitude, you can't feel anything else. As soon as you fill your consciousness with appreciation, you crowd out all lesser ideals. When you pack the available space with gratitude, negative emotions and negative feelings are instantly dislodged and set adrift. If you can feel at peace with only a few moments' commitment to gratitude, think what awaits you when you cultivate the habit of deliberate, conscious, everlasting gratitude! You become more attractive. You become more radiant. You release a vital energy that draws to you opportunities. Your life begins to work in a more orderly and creative way.

In your grateful heart, you can feel prosperity in relation to almost everything, so I would ask you to bless your car, your job, your family, the weather, the traffic, your place

Bless everything. Be thankful for everything.

of employment, the people you meet, your investments, your cash flow, your home, and your neighbors. Bless everything. Be thankful for everything. Experience gratitude as G-R–attitude, that is, God-realized attitude.

Without gratitude, you cannot keep from being dissatisfied with things as they are.

One of the ways that I cultivate this mindset is to keep a blessing bowl strategically located where I see it every day. Every time I walk by, it reminds me to be thankful, and I drop blessings in the bowl. Thank you for this today. Thank you for that today. I encourage you to come up with ways that help you develop a permanent attitude of gratitude. The truth is, there is no magical power over all the things you bless. It does not change them, but it does change YOU. Blessing the people and things around you makes an impact on your thoughts and feelings, which changes what you project into the world. The creative substance mirrors this projection of your thoughts and feelings in the form of events in your life. Remember the Law of Attraction? Because of this Law, your thanksgiving is more than a response to what is happening around you or to you. It is a causal energy, and it is an assurance of enduring blessings that will lead to personal prosperity for you.

Pay attention to what you are thinking. Pay attention to how you feel. Create in yourself the consciousness of gratitude. This practice will lead you to continual, deliberate, conscious creation. Without gratitude, you cannot keep from being dissatisfied with things as they are. The moment that you permit your mind to dwell with dissatisfaction upon things as they are around you, you will begin to lose ground. The grateful mind constantly fixes upon the best and continuously gives thanks. I have so perfected this practice that now, when something bad happens to me, I say, "Wow, look at the blessing in this!" I promise you that every time one door closes, another one opens, and it is bigger, better, greater. If you can look at everything in your life as an unending chain of blessings, you will be able to see the best, and create the best in your life.

Remember, gratitude is not a reactionary emotion. It is a causative energy. An abiding acknowledgment of the gifts in your life will bring you into a harmonious relationship with the good in everything, and then the good in everything will move toward you. We grow rich by thanksgiving; we grow impoverished by losing the spirit of gratitude. We have the choice to be great or the choice to be small, and when we are grateful, we are great. A monk, whose name was Brother David Steindl Rast, left us a wonderful quote, giving the entire formula for living a happy life: "Love wholeheartedly; be surprised; give thanks and praise; and then you will discover the fullness of your life."

At the end of this chapter, I have given you some very important exercises. They are meant to help you discover who you are and why you are here. How does this relate to gratitude? Buddha says that your job is to figure out what your job is, and then to do it

> **Remember, gratitude is not a reactionary emotion.**

with all your heart. Find your assignment. What do you want your grateful heart to begin attracting for you? Your life is your responsibility and you have to work at it. I commend you for diligently doing the work that you are doing as you read this book. You are stretching yourself every time you ask yourself a question and every time you look into yourself.

In the first part of EXERCISE 6, I want you to see your life as a tree. Draw the tree and label its different parts as the various elements of your life, as described below.

Next, list things that you are grateful for—just list them. As you build your gratitude list, I think you will find many, many things to be grateful for, perhaps even things that you never recognized or considered welcoming into your life before. Your list will become even more important as you start on the pathway to reclaiming yourself.

The last part of EXERCISE 6 is a questionnaire on dreams and what fills your heart. When you finish this exercise, look for recurring themes.

And most important of all, as you learn each component of the G.A.M.E.S. formula, remember to start incorporating it into your daily routine. Practice gratitude every day of your life, starting now.

Exercise 6:
Find the Blessing of You

PART 1: Your Tree of Life

Draw a tree with your life.

1. What do you see as the center of your life? Write this on the trunk of the tree.

2. Write on the roots what you feel your life is rooted to and grounded in.

3. Write on the branches what you feel are the main segments or most important people and areas of your life.

4. Write on the leaves what you desire to see blossom or bear fruit in your life.

PART 2: What Are You Grateful For?

_____

_____

_____

_____

_____

_____

_____

_____

_____

_____

_____

_____

_____

_____

_____

_____

_____

_____

_____

_____

_____

_____

_____

_____

_____

_____

_____

_____

PART 3: What Fills Your Heart?

1. What are your dreams? _____
_____
_____

2. If you could do or be anything, what would you do or be? _____
_____
_____

3. What is that thing in life that really does it for you?
_____
_____
_____

4. What is your purpose?_____
_____
_____

5. What do you love? _____
_____
_____

6. Do you know if you are doing the work you came here to do? _____
_____
_____

7. What do you really desire for life to unfold for you?
_____
_____
_____

8. What is it about who you are that you really want others to know?_____
_____
_____

9. If you knew you could not fail, what would you do?
_____
_____
_____

Chapter 7:
Assume the Attitude

W ho are you? The master or the slave? If you veered off your intended path because improper scripting misdirected you, then you most likely have a head full of unhealthy thoughts. But are you going to remain a slave to them for the rest of your life? Or are you going to make a stand and take your rightful place as the master of that cargo in your mind? Even if your prior scripting has so misguided you that you have disowned what you value most, you can still reclaim it.

It is through the reclamation process that we restore those disowned parts of ourselves and actively participate in the creation of our lives. You can design whatever reality you want for your own life. You can write your own script an create your own culture. Realize that you have an infin' abundance to draw from. The resources for building personal prosperity are limitless. So how can you reclaim what you disowned from the boundless possibilities available? Here is the crucial action you must take: acknowledge what it is that you are reclaiming.

That which you cannot acknowledge as true of yourself can never be fully realized.

Acknowledge, the "A" in G.A.M.E.S., is a simple principle, but it requires daily practice—as a matter of fact, it requires constant practice. What you must do is to imagine that you are already experiencing what you desire. This is called the Law of "As If." Imagine it "as if" you already have it. You must acknowledge the thoughts and the feelings of the desire or the wish fulfilled, until you have all of the sensory vividness of reality. That which you cannot acknowledge as true of yourself can never be fully realized. If you assume the feeling of fulfillment as if you already possess it, then this feeling crowds out all lesser ideals from your consciousness. As you recall, this is the same strategy we use with gratitude—leave space only for the attitudes that serve you. The dynamic Law of "As If" is extremely potent, because its scope involves all of the previous four Laws: the Law of Creative Thought, the Law of Focus, the Law of Responsibility, and the Law of Attraction.

I will give you an example from my own life to demonstrate the effectiveness of this acknowledgment "as if" technique. Several years ago, when I was in my sales organization, I taught workshops and the G.A.M.E.S. program periodically, through my seminar company. I wanted, however, to be speaking and teaching on a grander scale. In accordance with my desires of acquiring a bigger arena, I began operating under the Law of "As If." If people asked me what I did, I said, "I'm a motivational speaker, inspirational teacher, and author."

I had long admired Mr. Les Brown, a world-renowned speaker, author, and motivator, but I had never met him. Then, several years ago, I was calling entertainment companies to find an Elvis impersonator for my daughter's birthday party. I happened to get a wonderful gentleman on the phone, a comedian, who exchanged jokes with me in a jovial conversation. Apparently impressed with my quips, he asked what I did for a living. In the spirit of the moment, I answered from the Law of "As If," even though motivational speaking was not yet my primary source of income. When I explained that I was a motivational speaker, guess what happened! The gentleman told me to hold on a moment, and then he put me on a conference call with a third person, who was, himself, a speaker. At the end of our twenty-minute conversation, this speaker told me that he was doing an event in two days, and asked me to share the platform with him! Delighted, I accepted, and a few short months later, this same man was doing a church function with Les Brown. In spite of a host of obstacles that seemed destined to keep me away from Les, I engineered a scenario to meet with him and converse for a short time.

I was looking for Elvis and got Les Brown! Les has now become a good friend and mentor, and we have traveled nationally and internationally together, giving lectures on self-empowerment and speaking to large

> **Set aside time to identify what you really want.**

audiences. It was through practicing the Law of "As If" and having real belief that I created the opportunity to spend time with Les Brown and to achieve my "grandiose" plan.

I will give you another example of how this principle worked in my life, at a time long before I consciously used it. I have always loved horses. When I was in my late twenties, there was one particular breed that I loved, called the American Saddlebred. I became acquainted with a remarkable eighty-year-old gentleman from Illinois who had been an American Saddlebred trainer. His thrilling tales of past shows enthralled me. I was so consumed with images of his stories in my mind, that it was "as if" I had my own Saddlebreds and I was at the shows. Call it daydreaming, if you will, but I was actually utilizing the Law of "As If" unknowingly. First, I was holding these detailed mental visions, and the next thing I knew, I was in Kentucky at an auction, actually buying a Saddlebred! Six months later, I was in the show ring! Yes, I did get blue ribbons. I went on to show for almost ten years. I think we all unwittingly make use of these principles and laws. Don't dismiss such happenings as mere chance. You create events in your life, whether you know it or not.

Accept responsibility for your actions.

Set aside time to identify what you really want, focus on that, and imagine it as if you already have it. Miguel de Cervantes said, "Make it thy business to know thyself." This is not necessarily easy work. In fact, unearthing those precious buried parts of yourself, according to de Cervantes, "is the most difficult lesson in the world." To do this, it takes faith. It takes faith in yourself, it takes faith in your universe, and it takes faith in God. Remember, if you are not ready to live by this law consciously, you no doubt live by it unconsciously.

Look at your current situation in life, and recall what you were thinking about or doing several years ago. Accept responsibility for your actions and ask, "What thought processes did I harbor that helped create how I am situated today?" As you review the last few years, take an inventory of events and of what attitudes preceded them. It can be painful to accept responsibility for your own life, but magic arises from that acceptance. Once you take command of the power you already possess, you can claim your life, direct it, build it, and arrange it the way you want it to be. The key is knowing there is abundance for everyone. Your own personal prosperity depends upon disciplining your thoughts to welcome it into your life.

Are you getting used to the idea now that you are responsible for managing your life from here on out? Are you accepting the concept, but wondering how to begin the complex process of building the life you want? Great news for you: I have a clearly defined method that will help simplify setting about this task! I call it the "reclamation statement." Reclamation statements are the most powerful creative tool I have ever used. They can help manifest what you want in your life, because they put into action the laws you have learned, but don't require that you think about them! In *Think and Grow Rich,* Napoleon Hill refers to "conscious, deliberate attention, focused on your goals at all times." That is exactly what the reclamation statement does, and I will guide you in developing yours.

> A reclamation statement is a positive, present-day ownership statement that has an emotional charge for you.

A reclamation statement is a *positive, present-day ownership statement that has an emotional charge for you.* Let me break down the formula for you. First, it is *positive* and produc-

We want to think in terms of what we want, not what we don't want. For example, "I am full of vitality" (as opposed to "not easily tired").

Second, it is *present day* because we are using the Law of "As If." We want to think in terms of "I am," and "I have," as if it already exists for us—not as some remote future wish. For example, if you cherish in your imagination a lovely second home, build a reclamation statement as if it is already yours. One of my own statements is, "My family and I have a beautiful villa in Tuscany."

We want to think in terms of what we want, not what we don't want.

Third, the reclamation statement signifies *ownership*. It is yours, personally and uniquely. Remember that part of you once owned these desires, goals, or purposes, and then you disowned them. You are now reclaiming them from the heap of discarded treasures that are already yours. The statement does not have to have meaning or importance for anyone but you.

And last, your reclamation statement has an *emotional charge*. It has a feeling component to it, because feelings are as creative as thoughts. Find words that stimulate your emotions, that energize you, and that express what is inside you. You can create as many statements as you desire to see things manifest in your life.

Now, here is the crucial step by which you will bring magic to your life. Once you have identified your goals and built them into reclamation statements, take these statements and record them on an audiotape. Listen to this audiotape every day. Ideally, you will listen to your Reclamation Tape for twenty minutes every morning, thus setting the tone for the day. The strategy behind listening to the audiotape in your own voice is this: when you listen to something in your own voice as opposed to someone else's, the message bypasses conscious thinking and goes straight to nonconscious thinking, where it begins to facilitate change effortlessly.

As we have previously discussed, the nonconscious part of our thought processes creates at a higher ratio than does the conscious part. This Reclamation Tape can reach that deeper, central part of the creative thought process, and change your conscious and nonconscious thought. Because the tape is addressing your nonconscious mind, you can even perform other activities while listening to your tape! You will see real changes in your life as you attract and create those things you truly desire. Can you see the possibilities of taking the time to figure out exactly what you want, and then building it all—every facet of your life--into these statements?

The great secret is controlled imagination and well-sustained attention, firmly and repeatedly directed in your reclamation statements.

The great secret is controlled imagination and well-sustained attention, firmly and repeatedly directed in your reclamation statements. We need a defense against distractions. If we get hung up in not knowing what our goals are, or frazzled b formulating too many goals, or overwhelmed by the negat ity of our world, nothing gets deliberately created. Rem ber what I said about negative statements? They are si times more powerful than positive, productive ones. The Reclamation Tape is a system engineered to keep you out of distraction. We all need a system to keep us on track.

Recalling trigger switches can bring you back to center.

When you sit down to build your reclamation statements, go back over the exercises we have already done. Review what you have identified as dreams and goals, significant parts of your life, what makes you happy, and what draws you in and gives you purpose. As you are going through the information you have learned about yourself, some reclamation statements will evolve that are blanket, overall statements about your life. One of the statements on my tape is, "All my desires are fulfilled effortlessly." Your own statements can be about anything you want, including creating material things.

In addition to the blanket statements and the specific goal statements that you may include on your list, there will also likely be a couple of statements that just show up on your list without conscious effort, and which may not necessarily be goals. They may serve as messages of comfort or confirmations of faith. I call these "trigger switch" reclamation statements. They are important to memorize and use during times when you don't have easy access to your tape. If, for instance, you find yourself in a negative situation, or you are distracted or stressed, recalling trigger switches can bring you back to center, and help you stay focused on what you want.

One of the trigger switches that showed up among my reclamation statements, and that now rolls around in my head half e day, is, "God is my instant, constant, and abundant source supply and protection." Having this comment "mentally 'y" supplants anything negative I may encounter, such as distressing news stories or bothersome situations and circumstances that may otherwise sidetrack me. Another of my favorites is, "The essence of my life releases the God I love everywhere." Memorizing a few trigger switches can neutralize unwelcome situations. When you find yourself having feelings that don't suit you, just hit the switch in your mind.

I have worked with Reclamation Tapes for eleven years. One of my favorite stories about the successes of consciously creating from my tapes is the following: My first attempt at marriage was not the relationship that served my growth or my movement forward in this lifetime. When the marriage fell apart, I made the decision to bring about the type of relationship I really wanted. I spent a long time with me, analyzing what that looked like and how important it was, and I built fifteen reclamation statements on my ideal relationship. I listened to those statements as part of my tapes for three years before my current husband showed up in my life. I promise you, anybody who has met him can confirm that he is my perfect match, the love of my life. When I run down the inventory, he is fifteen out of fifteen! People used to ask, "What are you waiting for?" My answer was, "Well, this guy! I want this, and this, and this, and this." Then they would say, "Do you know what's wrong with you? Your expectations are too high." Maybe they were extremely high, but I got what I wanted!

Here are some details that illustrate what a fine match I **Magic becomes reality!** manifested. He took me to London to propose. We were married on a plantation built in the 1600s in Merita, Mexico. We flew down for the wedding, and then back to Fort Lauderdale the next weekend for the blowout party of the century. The party had a theme: it was called "Life is an Adventure." All the guests came dressed in white.

Remember to structure your statements in a positive way.

My groom and I were dressed in red. The first dance was a tango. The cake was in the shape of a mountain ridge with two planes soaring over. Then, we took off to Switzerland and Italy for two weeks—not too bad for somebody eating peanut butter out of a jar twelve years ago! The point is that you, too, can do or be anything. There are no limits to life, except the ones you make in your head. You can create your life as crazy-great as you want it to be. Don't tell yourself or anyone else that expectations are too high. Don't ever stop that magical thinking. Magic becomes reality!

Start working on composing your own statements. Think of this as building your life, because that is what it is. I suggest getting started by reviewing your O.W.L. goals in each category. For instance, take the section on health. Was one of your O.W.L. goals to eat healthier foods? If so, then work on a reclamation statement for this area of your life. What wording focuses your attention on what you do want to eat? What wording directs you to avoid distractions? What wording motivates you? For example, one of your reclamation statements for healthy eating may be, "I easily choose the right foods daily." Remember to structure your statements in a positive way. Don't use such terms as, "I won't do this or that." Also, don't equivocate. Commit yourself fully, without including contingencies or reasons why you are acting as your statement proclaims.

I have some things on my tape that I call "My Purpose." I have my search for God as part of my Reclamation Tape. One of my purpose statements is, "I am an agent of God in all that I do." I also have a section called, "More about Me, and a Little More about Me." You can use any categories you want, arrange them any way you want, and include anything that is important to you. Another great thing that reclamation statements can do is to change your habits. One of my personal examples of this is that I love to have things organized. However, I am always managing multiple tasks at once, and I haven't always been the most organized person. So, what did I do? I recorded on my tape the following statement: "I have an amazing system for organizing everything!" I built organization into my reclamation statements, and now everything has its place, and all of it stays organized. I was able to change a habit!

Decide which areas of your life you want to work on. How about, "My Career, My Money, My Finances"? If you are working on this aspect of your life, here is

The American dream of financial freedom is alive and doing well.

one thing I want you to know: the American dream of financial freedom is alive and doing well. There is so much misleading pessimism about how hard it is to make it, how difficult it is to succeed, and even that it's impossible to come up with anything new. I repeat: the American dream of financial freedom is alive and doing well. I want that thought in your head as you start building your statements.

There's a great story regarding advice that Andrew Carnegie, a staggeringly wealthy man, once gave Napoleon Hill. Carnegie told Hill to look in the mirror every day for thirty days, and to say something to the effect of, "I am going to make more money than Andrew Carnegie." Hill reports that the first time he did this, he looked back at himself in the mirror and said "Napoleon, you are a fraud." Carnegie told him to keep doing it. Hill followed the advice and persisted until h believed that he really would make more money than Carnegie. And what happened? He actually did! He created much more money than Andrew Carnegie, and helped other people create millions and millions of dollars.

When we have abundance and wealth, we can do the things we want to do.

As you start to work with some of your statements, you might at first feel like a fraud. Your Big Voice may say, "This isn't going to happen!" Some things will show up that you know are distinctly yours and that you want to record. Other things may not seem right for you. But write down even those goals that spit "I'm a fraud" back at you. And make a note of any negative conversations between Big Voice and Little Voice, because those inner arguments may represent cherished goals that are really struggling to get out. Look at these supposedly "fraudulent" dreams very closely, and you may find some of the most important disowned parts of you.

While building your statements, don't neglect the income statement. Let's face it, we all want to create revenue. When we have abundance and wealth, we can do the things we want to do. The creative substance loves specificity, so be as specific as possible, especially when it comes to areas like your income. The first income statement that I included on my Reclamation Tape years ago, said, "I have an annual income of $75,000 that continues to grow." I didn't want to put a cap on my earnings. Sure enough, my income began to grow incrementally, and before I knew it, I had created my goal: $75,000 per year. I raised my income statement accordingly, to $150,000 and then to $250,000. As my statement evolved upward, so did my earnings, and I eventually upped my statement to $500,000. I now have an income statement that says, "I have an annual income of ten million dollars that continues to grow." I also include a statement that says, "I tithe money, time, and ideas to people and places that make a real difference," because serving others is such an important calling for me.

As your mind expands to the possibilities, I grant you permission to get as big and bold as you can about what you want to create. Can you give yourself permission to set wildly outrageous goals? Can you give yourself permission to create what you really, really want? Here is another important question: once you give yourself permission to set high goals, can you then give yourself permission to achieve them? There is a subtle difference to grasp here. When you break through the barrier of thinking small and begin to think big, you also need to stop resisting getting the good things you deserve. If you think of "getting what you deserve" in terms of punishment or retribution, turn that idea around. Focus instead on the rewards life has to offer you. Acknowledge the abundance of the universe, and allow it to flow naturally to you.

To allow means "to grant fulfillment." Try granting yourself the fulfillment of your dreams. To allow also means "to make possible through a specific **We are entitled to enjoy and to play!**

action or through a lack of action." Take note of your feelings about what you deserve in life. Examine ways in which you may be blocking your own fulfillment. Trust that you deserve what you are consciously creating. Acknowledge the things you want "as if" you already have them, and then allow them to happen.

Don't feel guilty about creating and manifesting physical things. We are entitled to enjoy and to play! Build pleasure into your reclamation statements. Reclaim the glee you once had. A natural by-product of working with reclamation statements is that negative thoughts start to diminish without a struggle. I have listened to my tapes and paid attention to my thoughts for so many years, that I can stop midstream when a thought surfaces that is negative or that doesn't serve me. The tape works magic because it has a similar affect in keeping you out of distraction, and can eventually result in the habitual generation of thoughts that serve you.

Keep in mind that there is no prescribed set of goals or divisions for you to follow. The O.W.L. sheet is just an idea to get you started. Select any category you want—your needs may be completely different from any I have discussed. When you sit down and think about building your statements, just observe what shows up for you. Another tip: people tend to make run-on statements when they first start their tapes. But it is more effective to take one certain chunk and say, "I have this income." "I have this home." "I am this." Remember, the creative substance loves specificity.

In case you think that the reality of changing the way you "operate" is far-fetched, I want to point out a very concrete example of creating your own culture that comes from the business world. There are training companies that will hire into large corporations to change their corporate culture. In fact, corporations will spend $50,000 to $100,000 to change their corporate culture. Do you know why they do that? Because if they get all the employees thinking and behaving and maneuvering in the same way, they can create more revenue, a better bottom line, and an expanding company. You can change your personal culture in a similar way, through your Reclamation Tapes.

Here is a quick summary of how you will ultimately use

your reclamation statements. Write each of your goals in the format of a positive, present-day ownership statement that has an emotional charge. Record these statements on an audiotape. The first thing in the morning, pop in your tape and listen. Aim for twenty minutes of listening, and feel free to do other tasks at the same time. Even if you can spare only five minutes for your tape, though, your life will change. You can also use your tape throughout the day as your own personal motivator and energizer, when you need to regain your focus. Use the power of trigger switch reclamation statements when your tape is not available.

Remember that the G.A.M.E.S. strategy is to be done every day. You are already practicing gratitude every day. You will also begin daily acknowledgment of what you are reclaiming by constructing your statements. Later, after you learn more about the G.A.M.E.S. strategy, you will record your statements and listen to them. You can be confident that when you use these statements, you are using God's laws, the Laws of Life, timeless principles, in an action step. Now I'm going to challenge you. I want you to take the action step to begin composing your reclamation statements. Don't get caught up in your distractions. I want you to be using your reclamation statements productively, long after you finish this book. I dare you to get it done—I absolutely dare you!

Exercise 7:
Let the Reclamation Begin

PART 1: Treasure Box

Collect several magazines, a cardboard box (square gift boxes work well), scissors, and a glue stick. Find two hours of quiet time and listen to some soft favorite music, if you like. Go through the magazines and cut out anything that appeals to you. Don't think about which images are correct, or what they will look like together. Just put yourself on "autopilot" and choose what looks good at the moment. Once you have a significant number of pictures, glue them onto the box. When you are finished, you will have a "treasure box." The treasure box serves as a visual representation of your desires, dreams, and goals. Keep it where you will see it every day, and as you find other pictures that appeal to you, cut them out and keep them in the box. As this unconscious pictorial expression of you unfolds, you can use it to make more reclamation statements.

PART 2: Reclamation Statements

Begin to write your reclamation statements. You can have as many as you like. This is about you, for you. Remember the formula: a positive, present-day, ownership statement that has an emotional charge for you. Use the exercises that you have done so far to help you build your statements. We still have more information to cover before you finish writing and then record your tape, but for now, just get started composing your statements.

Chapter 8:
The Best Place
To Visit Every Day

W hen was the last time you traveled to a fascinating and refreshing destination? How long did it take you to make the journey? Did you want to return there soon after coming home? What if I told you that there is an enchanting spot available to you every single day? And that no matter who you are, where you are, or what your means are, you can travel to this place within moments, and you can return there over and over again as often as you like? If you think this is too good to be true, I can only encourage you to see for yourself. This miraculous site lies within yourself, and you go there by way of meditation. **Meditate** is the "M" in the G.A.M.E.S formula.

Management consultants have come to view meditation as an effective stress management technique. Scientists speak of it in terms of brain hemispheres, and spiritual seekers view it as a pathway to God. Artists look to it as a way to achieve higher creative insights. All of this is true. However, there is more. We meditate to discover our own identity, our right and fitting place, and our personal truth. It is the gateway to ourselves—our wholeness, our power, and our creativity. Through this practice, we link to our inner source and our intrinsic wisdom; in turn, through this connection, we can facilitate changes to our outer world.

Our culture does not teach us how to be silent.

Your prior notions of meditation may conjure up images of robed monks in an isolated monastery, ascending to a state of awareness that is unattainable by the average person. I want to assure you there is nothing complicated about meditation. It is a simple technique that requires no special planning or advanced training. It is as natural as closing your eyes. Anyone can meditate and enter a space that is both stimulating and relaxing at the same time. This space has always existed within the silence of your own mind, and is readily accessible, whether you have chosen to open the door or not. I can't emphasize enough the value of this experience and the consequences of becoming aware of your own silence. I have meditated for close to thirty years, and I believe it is as essential as taking a breath of air or drinking a glass of water.

Our culture does not teach us how to be silent, and we don't appreciate the value of silence. Why do we often feel compelled to fill quiet times alone with some kind of noise, with music or television? When you are on an elevator with people you don't know and everyone is quiet, what do you do? You look the other way; you look at the floor; you look at the ceiling. What happens when you are riding in a car or eating dinner with others and the conversation comes to a halt? Do you feel uncomfortable? Why are these moments awkward for so many of us? We have no training in silence. And it's not just outside noise. We keep a constantly running inner dialogue, just like the outer dialogue. Remember the Big Voice/Little Voice conversations that we previously explored? It is that chatter that keeps us away from our creative selves. What if you could delve beneath the chatter, that ongoing barrage of directions and advice and warnings that you continually give yourself in your head? What if you could glide beyond all that and immerse yourself in the serene surroundings of silence? I promise that you can.

See what others from different walks of life have had to say about the impact of chatter versus silence. Theodore Roethke, American poet and Pulitzer Prize winner, said, "A mind too active is no mind at all." Pythagoras, **Meditation can provide physical benefits.** a Greek philosopher and mathematician who lived between 580 and 500 BC, studied the relationship of mathematics to weights and measures and to musical theory. He said, "Learn to be silent. Let your quiet mind listen and absorb." Blaise Pascal, a French philosopher, scientist, and mathematician who made major contributions to the fields of hydraulics and pure geometry, commented, "All man's miseries derive from not being able to sit quietly in a room alone." There is a quote I came across from a physicist, Fritjof Capra, which says, "During periods of relaxation, quiet time after concentrated intellectual activity, the intuitive mind seems to take over and can produce sudden clarifying insights." And, of course, the benefits of experiencing and using silence have been emphasized in religious writings. You may associate this practice with Eastern spirituality, but in fact, references to silence are widespread in scriptures from across the globe. Here is one from Psalms 4:4: "Commune with your own heart upon your bed, and be silent."

Symptoms of anxiety, tension, and premenstrual syndrome have all shown improvements with meditation.

Now I want to satisfy some WIIFM's. Do you know what a WIIFM is? It's a question that we often ask: What's In It For Me? Here's the answer to your first WIIFM in regard to meditation: physical benefits. That's right, meditation can provide physical benefits, and many of these have been documented in medical literature.

First and foremost, meditation has been shown to decrease stress, a culprit that may contribute to as much as 95 percent of all disease. Numerous studies have shown meditation to be beneficial in the reduction of stress as perceived by the participants, often with measurable reduction in bodily functions related to stress, such as blood pressure and cortisol (a hormone increased during stress) levels. Many studies have suggested a beneficial relationship between meditation and heart disease, particularly in regard to the stress reduction it offers. Symptoms of anxiety, tension, and premenstrual syndrome have all shown improvements with meditation in various studies.

In a review article published in 2003 in *The Journal of the American Board of Family Practice,* several mind-body therapies were evaluated, including meditation, relaxation, imagery, hypnosis, and biofeedback. The reviewers concluded that, "There is now considerable evidence that an array of mind-body therapies can be used as effective adjuncts to [that is, used in combination with] conventional medical treatment for a number of common clinical conditions." Conditions that were examined in this study included, among others, cardio-vascular disease, chronic pain, insomnia, and arthritis.

Some studies have suggested that meditation can improve the immune system and even slow the aging process! In summary, although meditation cannot take the place of conventional medical therapy, there is mounting evidence that with regular practice, it can benefit health in a variety of ways.

There are numerous other mental and physical benefits that, although difficult to quantify, are nonetheless quite obvious to those who meditate daily. Some of these are an enhanced sense of wellbeing, increased energy levels, higher produc-tivity, and greater creativity. More satisfying relationships occur because you have learned to communicate with your-self. There is a closer connection to yourself and a closer con-nection to God.

Are you beginning to understand that meditation has genuine relevance for your life? If you are unfamiliar with the prac-tice, you may feel resistance toward this avenue of self-exploration. However, if you will give it a chance, I think you will quickly appreciate the difference it can make in the quality of your life.

Now I want to share with you some differ-ent types of meditation techniques—all of which are easy and straightforward. There **Listen to your own thoughts.** are many more methods than I will discuss here, but keep in mind that all of them are merely routes to silence. In the same way that different people choose different types of exercise, different people will prefer different techniques of meditation. I have practiced many types, and those I am presenting here are the ones I have found most useful and practical.

Even five minutes of silence with yourself can make an enormous difference. Here is a simple, quick meditation to introduce you to letting silence prevail. Turn off the television and the radio. Sit in a comfortable position, close your eyes, and for five minutes just be with yourself in your own mind. Listen to your own thoughts. Set down the book right now and try it.

After these moments in silence, journal your thought process. What was that like? Did you feel that it was the longest five minutes of your life? Was there a lot of chatter going on? Did you hear your inner voice saying, "It has to be five minutes by now"? How did you feel afterward? Refreshed? Relaxed? Peaceful? In the beginning, you may be uncomfortable with the silence, but do it anyway. Even five minutes of silence with yourself can make an enormous difference.

Another form of meditation is something called "visualization." In this method, you will generate a picture in your mind, and then allow the picture to go wherever it wants. This will probably take three to four minutes. It would be ideal if someone could read this section to you while you focus on the voice guiding you through. If not, just read through this section and then pause to visualize what I describe.

Close your eyes and begin by picturing an elevator door. Push the button to call the elevator. As the door opens and you enter the elevator, you see that it is an absolutely beauti-ful elevator, built just for you. This is your elevator. Now hit the very, very, very top button. Feel the elevator start to move up. As the elevator is moving, you are just being with the elevator and letting it transport you. You get to the very top, and the door opens. Step out into a magnificent space. This is your space, a sacred space. It can be indoor or outdoor, a building, a room—any place you want it to be, because it is yours, arranged just for you. You can return here any time you want. It was created just for you.

As you walk through this sacred space, you see a huge, comfy couch. Walk to it and sit down. As you relax on the couch, you notice the exquisite beauty of this place. As you con-tinue to look around, you realize there is an envelope nearby, and it has your name on it. Reach over and pick up the enve-lope. Now open it. Inside that envelope is a message just for you. Read the message. Keep that message with you, and look around again, soaking in every detail of this spot that has been created just for you. Now stand up and take one last look around. Walk back to the elevator and push the button. When the door opens, get on, push the down button, and see the door close. Feel the elevator come back down to the ground floor. Allow the door to open. Now walk out of the elevator and as you do, open your eyes.

There may be a gift for you in that visualization. Sometimes the note is a message for you that becomes a reclamation statement or a trigger switch reclamation statement. You can use the same visualization to get inside your own mind. Talk yourself through it, and then let go and see where it leads. You can record any type of visualiza-

Visualizations are a very effective form of meditation.

tion that you like onto a cassette, and listen to it. You can have somebody else record it for you. There are many different ways to use visualization. In the past, when I wanted an answer for something, I would visualize in detail going to get one of my teachers, and having them come and sit down with me. Then I would ask the question I needed answered and wait for his or her response. Visualizations are a very effective form of meditation, and yet just one of many from which to choose.

Make room in your life for spending time outdoors. My own personal favorite type of meditation is something called a quantum, or a sacred sound, a method that is similar to chanting. I like singing a sacred sound called the Hu. The word "Hu" is an ancient Sanskrit name for God. So when you sing the Hu, you are singing, in essence, a love song to God. Often, after singing the Hu for a period of time, you will be able to hear a sound coming back to you, and it has been said that this is God singing back to you. After almost thirty years of singing the Hu, this happens naturally to me. Sometimes, I will be in a conversation, and I will stop and say, "Hold on," because I hear this beautiful sound ringing in my ears. Likewise, even in the middle of a busy mall, I can achieve silence by singing the Hu in my head. It is a very powerful, sacred sound.

Experiment with this method by doing it for yourself. Hu is an elongated sound, (H-u-u-u-u-u). It has a tonal quality like a musical note and is pronounced like the man's name, Hugh. Pause a moment here, close your eyes, and sing the Hu five times. What effect does it have on you?

I also recommend that you try listening to professionally recorded meditation tapes and audio CDs that can be purchased from a number of stores, including Borders, and Barnes and Noble. There are thousands of choices. I happen to be particularly fond of Deepak Chopra's tapes. Such tapes are excellent for exploring ways to get to silence.

Other activities also constitute meditation. Nature has its own way of gently quieting our thoughts. Take time to stroll on the beach, go to the park, walk in the woods, or watch a sunrise or sunset. I urge you to make room in your life for spending time outdoors. Nothing can replace nature as a pathway to perspective and reflection. Stand by the ocean and just take in a breath. It is a way of freeing yourself from chatter, and experiencing the silent mind.

There are also innumerable types of breathing exercises. One is a yoga breath, a type of meditation that will allow you to arrive at silence in your mind, even in the hectic onslaught of a maddening world. Here is the way to experience it: place your tongue on the roof of your mouth, right behind your teeth, and breathe in through your nose for a count of four; hold the breath for a count of seven; breathe out through your mouth for a count of eight. Go through this series four times, which will take two minutes or less. This inconspicuous form of meditation is appropriate for any setting—even a bustling train station or a difficult board meeting that frazzles your nerves. Just take your counted breaths, allow yourself to get to that silent spot, and remain collected even if those around you are rattled. Try it for yourself right now.

Another method I want you to try is the morning meditation journal. This is a writing activity that will help you sort and discard the junk in your own mind. Here's how it works: when you get up

Discard the junk in your own mind.

in the morning, before you do anything else, write in your journal, and keep writing until you have four pages filled. It doesn't matter in the least what you write—just move your hand across the page and write whatever comes to mind. For example, you might find yourself saying, as you are trying to get through all of the pages, "I hate doing this journal. I am too tired. I have work to do." Write that down! Anything that comes into your head—just keep writing, keep writing, keep writing, until your four pages are completed.

Just keep writing. As you write, your Big Voice will pop in with all of its negative comments. Eventually, though, your creative Little Voice will come out with wisdom, insight, creativity, and your own personal truth. Such a result is exactly what this type of meditation is designed to do—to guide you through the muck and the mire of your own mind, finally uncovering you. Try this technique when you wake up tomorrow. Remember, you have to keep writing past the point of your resistance, for this is the point at which the inner you will, at last, reveal itself to the outer you. Write until you have finished four pages—and no cheating—they have to be standard-size pages!

The last form of meditation I will describe is one that has been the most eye opening for many of my coaching clients and students. What this method involves is setting up an evening of silence. This means no television, no radio, no cell phone, no beeper, no Internet, no conversation—just you and your journal. You must be with you alone for an entire evening, journaling whatever shows up in the experience, including good thoughts, bad thoughts, ideas, scripting . . . anything and everything. Continue to journal well past your point of personal comfort. Just keep writing. You will eventually reach what can be called "stream of consciousness."

It is here that you may discover amazing truths, words of wisdom, and personal treasures. People usually have "aha!" insights when they commit to this evening of silence.

It is worthwhile to expend effort arranging such an evening, even if it is difficult because of children, family, or business obligations. I urge you to find a way to bring about this night of silence and journaling with no distractions. You can experience astounding insights. I have encountered many, many, people who tried this exercise once and were so impressed with the results that they now schedule regular silent evenings alone.

This silence exercise is one of the most powerful exercises I believe you will do. It can demonstrate that you carry your own splendid wisdom and that you need to allow space for it to emerge. During this silent evening, you can also work on reclamation statements. Bear in mind that you should write in your journal even the negative thoughts that show up while you are in silence. It is crucial to examine what is shouting at you, saying, "No, you can't do it," or "No, I am in fear." Many people tend not to write down the negative, because they think if they document it, then they will create it. This is not the case! To the contrary, first you must take a look at it to be able to "uncreate" it.

An evening of silence is a fine opportunity to recharge your batteries. After some practice with it, you will realize that there is a distinction between quiet and silence. Silence is what happens after you get past striving for quiet. It is something even deeper than quiet. Many people get discouraged when they

Silence is what happens after you get past striving for quiet.

can't quiet the chatter in their minds. Don't worry about the torrent of thoughts that invades your mind when you start to meditate. Realize that you don't have to quiet or quell that stream. You will eventually be able to dip down beneath the stream and find the silence of a meditative state. Once you start practicing the silence and getting accustomed to it, the flow of ideas—as opposed to daily chatter—starts bubbling up and becoming rich and valuable. Often, with me, the ideas flood so fast that I know they are coming from a higher place. We all have that ability to tap into the place of inner wisdom and personal power, and the way to do it is through silence.

Find a pathway to that silent part of your mind on a daily basis. We have discussed some diverse ways to meditate. I highly recommend that you try these various methods and determine which is the best fit for you. You may want to use different methods on different days, or you may find one or more that suit your needs more aptly than the rest. Whatever means you settle on, I encourage you to find a pathway to that silent part of your mind on a daily basis. The benefits of meditation will amaze you. I once listened to Deepak Chopra give an amusing interview. Wayne Dyer kept coming up with scenarios and asking him what he would do in that situation. To each question, "What would you do?" Deepak kept answering, "Meditate." His solution to every problem was to meditate! St. Frances de Sales says, "Half an hour's meditation is essential, except when we are busy, then a full hour is needed."

Meditation is an important part of your G.A.M.E.S. formula. You have learned the Laws of Life. You understand the consciousness of gratitude. You understand that you need to consciously acknowledge what you want to create in your life. Now you will add making a place in your life for being silent. Once you have found the wisdom, the comfort, and the perspective that lives, always, so conveniently located in your own self, you will want to become a regular visitor to the site.

> *What lies beneath us and what lies before us are tiny matters compared to what lies within us.*
> **—Ralph Waldo Emerson**

Exercise 8:
Explore the Voice of Your Heart—Silence

For one evening: no television, no radio, no conversation, no distraction. Keep a journal with you, and note everything in your inner dialogue. At some point, journal for as long as you can, staying in your stream of consciousness.

Chapter 9:
A Feast for Mind and Body

ogether we have explored thoughts and scripts, dreams and decisions, intentions and attitudes—powerful mental and emotional concepts, but nonetheless intangible. Because we cannot see or touch or hear the landscape of the mind, it's easy to imagine that part of ourselves to be disconnected from the physical self. What is your concept of the mind? Do you think of it as existing in a fixed relationship with your body, maybe housed in flesh, but not really joined with it?

As vital as it is to work on the processes of the mind that we have discussed, this work, alone, is not sufficient for a rewarding life. We also need to create the health, well-being, and vitality to enjoy the dreams that we make come true. We must learn how to become active participants in energizing our whole being, including physical and mental aspects. **Energize** is the "E" in G.A.M.E.S

Many of us shortchange the most basic elements that energize our health and well-being. What are these crucial starting points? Eating right and exercising. It sounds simple, but why is it so hard to do the right thing when it comes to caring for our bodies? A major barrier to carrying out our plans for exercise routines and healthy eating is a flaw in our thought processes. We tend to think of the body as a compartment that is partitioned off from the mind, with no significant interchange between the two. But in fact, our conspicuous, noisy, active bodies share "wiring" with the invisible workings of our minds.

I am describing what you may have heard referred to as the "mind-body connection." So what? So the mind and body are interconnected. What does that mean in regard to your daily life? It means that you need to look at your thoughts, emotions, and beliefs in terms of your physical health. Deepak Chopra expresses it this way: "Your immune system and every cell in your body eavesdrops on every belief, mood, thought, and feeling." Ask yourself this question: are your mental/emotional patterns currently supporting your health, or interfering with it?

This may be a complex question, and one that you have no ready answer for. Let's explore it by breaking it down into more specific questions: Just exactly how do you view your own body? What are your thoughts about your physical being? What is its purpose? How does it function? How do you interpret signs and signals from your body? Do you view your body as a vehicle by which you can move around and perform daily tasks, much like your car?

As you reflected on the answers to these questions, did you detect any tendency to regard your body as something mechanical, something that is untouched and unaltered by the mind? Are your nonconscious thoughts conveying a sense that the body is not related to those intangible thoughts and dreams and attitudes we discussed? The truth is that the mind and body are intimately coupled, impinging on each other in the most direct way. They mesh like the cogs on the gears of a clock, perpetually driving each other.

We are scripted to what our health may be and how we may age, just like we are scripted in other ways. For example, if your father died from heart disease, you may carry the thought through your adulthood that inevitably you will die from heart disease, thus increasing this likelihood just by your thought process. How can this be? Because your body is not merely a physical device. It communicates with the mind and is molded by the attitudes and beliefs of the mind.

Are you seeing the rest of your life, in relationship to your body, as a time of progressive deterioration? This is the view of aging that we generally absorb from our culture. A valid alternative to this perspective is to see aging as an opportunity for greater wisdom, love, creativity, meaning, and joy. Instead of succumbing to the idea that the years carry you passively past your prime, commit to meeting the successive stages of your life with active renewal and increased mental and physical capacity.

Deepak Chopra has this to say on the subject of aging: "You can reverse your biological age by changing your perceptions. Perceptions create reality. By changing your perceptions, you change your reality. By changing the perception of your body, over time you can reverse your biological age." What exactly does this mean to you? This means that you can take an active, conscious role in creating your health, your vitality, and your well-being. Put another way, you influence the way you feel. Because of the mind-body connection, you are influencing how you feel right now. But are you deliberately influencing it in a positive way, or are you, by default, letting negative thought processes adversely affect the way you feel? Once you accept responsibility for the way you feel, you can use your reclamation statements to enhance your physical well-being. Build statements relating to your body that encourage and promote good health all the time.

You may have a hard time accepting the notion that you really can influence your body and your health to any significant degree. The body appears static or solid to us because changes occur very slowly. In reality, however, your physical body is in a constant state of turnover and renewal. The vast majority of your cells undergo a cycle of death and replacement many times throughout your lifetime. For example, the lining of your stomach is replaced every four to eight days. Your fingernails grow out completely within about six months. Your red blood cells live for approximately four months before they die and get replaced. In an even more elementary way, the very atoms and molecules that compose your body are in a constant state of flux with those of your environment. Over the course of your lifetime, the chemical compounds that make up "you" come and go repeatedly. Is there any wonder that with such a fluid state of being, our bodies can be influenced by many factors, both external and internal?

I want to make one point perfectly clear: being aware of the mind-body connection does not mean that you should forgo regular checkups. I am not endorsing your own personal health care plan as a substitute for medical care, but as a powerful tool you can use to enhance your own well-being. I want to describe for you an experience from my own life. I had some health issues and sought medical advice. I underwent the suggested tests. All appeared fine, and I was waiting on one more result. Then I received that unbelievable call that said, "Kandee, you have cancer." My head reeled; I was four days away from leaving on my honeymoon to Europe. But I knew the best thing I could do was to keep my thought processes in good order.

I refused to get into the "why now?" or "why me?" conversation in my head. I chose to stay in my beliefs, the thoughts, and the attitudes that best served me. I took all of the proper precautions and follow-up tests and quickly found out that surgery was the option of choice. I redid my Reclamation Tape with a heavy emphasis on healing and recovery. I went on my honeymoon and left any scary thoughts behind. I came home to surgery, listening to my tape every day, even taking it with me to the hospital. All of my doctors and surgeons were amazed at my speedy recovery. They all said the same thing: I had a great attitude, and it was my attitude that helped facilitate my recovery. And I will tell you that I maintained that attitude by listening to my tape every day. Our thoughts are so powerful and in this crazy world full of distraction, we need a way to "hold the course." Today, I am cancer free and feeling great.

You can influence your health by the choices you make. The thoughts, attitudes, and intentions you choose to harbor affect your physical well-being, and in turn, the way you treat your body influences your mental and emotional state. Now that you are beginning to realize the far-reaching implications that adjustments to your mind or body have, it will be easier for you to develop and maintain healthy habits. Following is a list of basic rules for good health, to practice on a daily basis. Consider incorporating these ideas into your Reclamation Tapes. Remember: by changing your thoughts, you can change your body. Your health is your responsibility.

	Basic Rules for Good Health
1.	Eat a well-balanced diet.
2.	Eat only when hungry.
3.	Crave fresh fruits and vegetables.
4.	Drink pure water as your main beverage.
5.	Avoid processed foods.
6.	Create a feeling of well-being by exercising and craving it.
7.	Have the energy to exercise.
8.	Get plenty of rest.

Here are some additional points to take a look at in relation to your own physical being: How do you receive communication from your body? What is the intelligence of your body telling you? When you are tired, do you give yourself caffeine or another stimulant to stay awake late? Do you have that same stimulant in the morning to jump-start your day because you didn't get enough rest to begin with? Do you work all day and ignore signs of hunger and the need to eliminate, because you are too busy? Do you overeat past the point of being full? Do you take time to explore troublesome feelings? Or do you just mask them with antidepressants, alcohol, or food?

Just as we are learning to differentiate between our Big Voice and our Little Voice, we can now begin to pay attention to our body's voice. What is it requesting? What does it need? Have we been ignoring an important request? Start to listen to the signals from your body and honor those that promote good health. Most of the time, you already know which ones are good for you and which ones are not.

It is of paramount importance for you to educate yourself about your own physical being. It is your responsibility to learn how you function. Do you take the time to learn about you? Do you take the time to learn the right foods to eat, the right type of nutritional supplements to take, the right exercise that works for you? Or do you just go to the doctor with every ache and pain and say, "Fix me"? At the other extreme, do you merely live with the aches and pains and discomforts, without taking the time to learn how to heal them? You are your responsibility, and you can combine outside learning and medical advice with your inner knowledge to become the expert on you. In the following paragraphs, I will discuss some specific ways you can energize yourself. As you read through these suggestions, think in terms of how you can customize them for yourself.

Educate yourself about your own physical being.

Observe how much processed food you and your family consume and make the decision to enjoy only whole, fresh foods. Your body and its cells are alive. Why would you want to feed it essentially "dead" fuel? Much of the food that is readily available to us is overprocessed. In our society today, we have an epidemic of obesity and illness. It is my personal belief that much of the problem arises from overprocessed food. It is our choice and our responsibility to put good things into our bodies.

Exercise your responsibility to find ways to fit in your rest and recovery time.

Pay attention to your breathing. Sometimes we move so fast that we are not even catching a real breath. Use the breathing meditation. Learn to enjoy a breath—a deep, real breath that fills your whole being. Be mindful of the vital way each inhalation nourishes your physical self, and how each exhalation rids yourself of waste products.

A restful mind and a rested body generate creativity and renewal. Real recovery time promotes vitality and energy. What does recovery time mean? It means having time away from whatever you are doing to rejuvenate. I don't just mean adequate sleep and rest; it is more than that. It is finding whatever works for you to recover. For instance, it may be a massage or going to a movie. It may mean time with your spouse or children, playing with the dog, or reading a good book. It may be a walk on the beach or by a lake. Getting adequate recovery time requires paying attention to how hard you push yourself and knowing when to slow down.

When I first started to understand what rest and recovery time truly meant, I was in my sales organization, and I was that 24/7 person. You could call me anytime, day or night. I changed after spending time with a mentor and coach who taught me about real recovery time. I modified my schedule from a seven-day workweek down to a five-day workweek. In three months I doubled my income, due to the power of rest and real recovery time. Exercise your responsibility to find ways to fit in your rest and recovery time.

Seek out time in every day for some kind of physical activity. Walk, stretch, move. Movement alone can stimulate your mind and body. I ask you not to take this lightly. We know that we need exercise to keep our bodies strong and limber, but the effects of movement, activity, and working out are much more far-reaching. Remember those gears of the mind and body driving each other? Whenever we perform physical activity, we engage those gears. We activate the mind as well as the body; the mind, in turn, further activates the body. There are so many ways to get the physical activity that you need. Find one or two of them and get started, as part of your everyday G.A.M.E.S. formula for life.

The final item I want to discuss on the list of elements that energize is perhaps the most important, and one you may never have considered. This item is love, an essential component in fueling your health and well-being. Love is the essence of life. For human beings, love is as essential as food and water; without it, we can't survive. A friend who was also a chiropractor and holistic physician once said to me, "You want to know what the Fountain of Youth is? It is love. If I could bottle those endorphins that are fired from being in loving activities, it would be the Fountain of Youth." Love lets you know that you are alive. It motivates you to do great things. Through the power of love, you rekindle forgotten energies. You tap into unknown parts of yourself.

> **Through the power of love, you rekindle forgotten energies.**

Love is not just a psychological experience; love actually transforms biology. Research in the 1990s showed us that loneliness, or involvement in relationships that are hostile or have poor communication, can damage the body's cardiovascular and immune systems. Studies also show that people with life-threatening diseases experience significant recovery in support groups.

Think about love. Talk about love. Seek out love. Make love. Encourage love. For three decades, the small town of Roseta, Pennsylvania, was studied for its occupants' unusually high incidence of good health and increased longevity. The findings pointed to the fact that there were remarkably close family and community ties. Roseta is a prime example of the healing power of nurturing. It also shows us that day-to-day dialogue with loved ones can be a life-sustaining force.

Be always conscious of your loving, caring, and nurturing activities. Think about love. Talk about love. Seek out love. Make love. Encourage love. Commit yourself to expressing love in every interaction of your life. Let your healing love nurture you and the world around you. Make love the most important thing you do. Remember, when you have the choice between a loving or non-loving thought or action, choose the loving one.

What can you do to be sure that how you think and feel actually supports your health and healing? I recommend taking the time to reread and rethink the questions I have put forth in this chapter. Thoroughly examine your attitudes about the mind-body connection. You almost certainly have experienced the way anxious or frightening thoughts can create uncomfortable physical feelings. Why don't you try testing out the positive? See how focusing on thoughts that serve you make your body feel. And start noticing the reverse—how physical activity, such as biking or running—and recovery time—such as a walk in nature or a massage—can uplift your thoughts and moods

Once you establish solidly within your beliefs that the mind-body connection is real, you will have gone a long way toward energizing yourself. Appreciating the implications of this link enables you to stick to healthy eating and exercise plans more easily and naturally. Recovery time becomes an essential rather than a luxury. Seeing love as the ultimate energizer can motivate you to cultivate it and make it part of what you do every moment.

> Carry within you a new respect for the mind-body connection.

Your daily G.A.M.E.S. practices at this point include gratitude, acknowledgment of that which you are reclaiming, meditation, and now energizing. Beginning today, carry within you a new respect for the mind-body connection and the implications of this bond.

Exercise 9:
Energize Your Reclamation Statements

Continue to work on your reclamation statements. Review all of the work you have done so far to help generate some more statements for you. Use this chapter on energizing to write statements that are directly related to the renewing of your body.

Chapter 10:
We Can Live in the Wisdom of Uncertainty

To have anything in this physical universe, you must have the intention and the desire to create it. You must also have faith, an innermost knowing, that what is expected will come true. To have faith, you must give up attachment to the thing you desire. You are probably thinking, "But you've just convinced me to take the time and effort to pinpoint what is in my heart, rewrite my scripts, change my thought processes, and consciously acknowledge what I want. Now you're telling me not to be attached to what I want?!" Yes! That is exactly what I'm telling you.

Attachment is the enemy of achievement. It comes from poverty-consciousness, and it actually keeps us prisoners of hopelessness, mundane needs, trivial concerns, quiet desperation, and seriousness. These are characteristics of a mediocre life. When you dare to be remarkable, you begin by uncovering your true self. Your unquestioning belief in the power of your true self grants you detachment. Fear and insecurity arise from not knowing your true self and its might. Attachment, in turn, is the product of this insecurity. When you experience attachment, you cling to what you want out of distrust that it will become or remain yours.

Within uncertainty is the freedom to know that you can create the life you want.

In contrast, when you experience detachment, there is no need to hold on so tightly, because you have the faith, or the knowing, that your desires will be created to your highest and best good. Remember, the richness of your life is in direct proportion to your willingness to be in your own discovery. The intention of your desire and the attention that you place on it, combined with detachment, is the quickest way to achieve your dreams. In other words, know what you want and that you will have it, and then surrender. The "S" in G.A.M.E.S. refers to your ability to **Surrender.** It signifies your faith in the grace and order of the universe.

How, you may ask, can I have faith that I can have anything I want, when I look around and observe the uncertainty of life? The answer is that it is from that very uncertainty that all the possibilities exist, that all your potential triumphs arise. Ground yourself in the wisdom of uncertainty. Live in faith of the knowledge that all will be provided for you. Within uncertainty is the freedom to know that you can create the life you want. The wisdom of uncertainty is a fertile ground of pure creativity and real freedom.

I want to tell you a story from my life that illustrates how you can have deep faith that your wants will be fulfilled, while at the same time, not be attached to an outcome. When my daughter Katie was small, we lived on the east side of the city and Katie went to school on the west side. For six years, I drove two to two-and-one-half hours a day, because I wanted her in a certain environment. Finally, we bought a house on the west side, and they moved the school east! With the new location, I still had to drive two-and-one-half hours, and it was even worse traffic than before.

With what I know about the Laws of Life and being grounded in the wisdom of uncertainty, I chose not to be upset. Instead, I held the belief, "A solution will manifest." Then, one day when I was on the campus, one of the school administrators said to me, "I just want to let you know that we have a new service. A bus will be coming into your neighborhood to pick up your daughter." That was good news! Then, do you know what she added? "The bus will be stopping on the corner of your street." There is real power in having faith that the world just works out the way it is supposed to, in matters small and large.

Faith is confidence in the integrity of the natural order and the infallibility of its laws.

What is faith? Faith is confidence in the integrity of the natural order and the infallibility of its laws. Faith is an abiding trust that all is in right order, because it is governed and protected by superlative powers that will not fail. Faith is the master key to great discovery, invention, and achievement. Belief is of the intellect, but faith is of the soul. Napoleon Hill says that faith is the head chemist of the mind. He describes it this way: when faith blends with thought, the subconscious mind instantly picks up the vibration, translates it into its spiritual equivalent, and transmits it to infinite intelligence. He also says that all thoughts that have been emotionalized or given feeling, and mixed with faith, begin immediately to translate themselves into their physical equivalent, or counterpart.

Will you listen to your own heart, your own truth, no matter which way it leads you?

Many people mistakenly think about what they want in terms that work counter to this principle. Take, for example, the person who says, "If I just had enough money in the bank, then I would be happy." This person is chasing the illusion of security and demonstrating his attachment to the outcome, without surrendering to the process. Behind this wish is a Big Voice whispering, "I don't have faith in my ability to consciously create. I need to be shown that it works before I put faith in it." But this is contrary to what faith is all about! Having faith implies NOT having to be shown. Hence, such wishes block your own creative process. It does not work without the magical elixir of faith.

When an individual lacks faith in life in general, he or she is like a plane without a rudder being tossed about in the wind. This condition is not conducive to creating health or happiness. Take some time to answer the following questions for yourself: Do you have faith in you? What or whom are you faithful to? What do you have faith for? We can have faith for our lives, our relationships, our loves, our belief systems.

The fact is that faith requires us to relinquish control; also, faith requires that we trust. Most of us have inner dreams that we can uncover if we have the courage to take a look, spend time with ourselves, and then accept them. Then we must have the faith to act on what we have discovered. Remember O.W.L. To thine own self be true. What do you want? Do you have the willingness to do whatever it takes? Will you listen to your own heart, your own truth, no matter which way it leads you?

Jesus recognized faith as a great attribute of the human soul. Being aware of its power and its magnitude, he said, "If ye have faith as a grain of mustard seed, ye shall say unto the mountain, remove hence to yonder place, and it shall remove, and nothing shall be impossible to you." Jesus declared many times that faith was absolutely essential in the many remarkable healings of his ministry. Faith removes limitations. Faith is the greatest transforming power of all life, and it brings, in its wake, the divine inheritances of health, happiness, joy, and a more abundant life.

How do we cultivate faith? Faith is a state of mind that can be created by repeated instructions to the subconscious mind. You can convince the subconscious mind that you believe you will receive that which you are asking

Rely upon faith to provide realities not yet present in consciousness.

for, and it will act upon that belief. The subconscious mind passes back to you that belief in the form of faith, your personal knowing. You can develop the state of faith in much the same way as you develop the attitudes you seek in your reclamation statements. Napoleon Hill says, "Repetition of affirmation of orders to your subconscious mind is the only known method of voluntary development of the emotion of faith." Rely upon faith to provide realities not yet present in consciousness. Develop the habit of using faith to supply the inspiration and courage to move ahead with your precious dreams, even when there is no tangible evidence that you will achieve them.

When you are considering a course of action, things will start to show up that let you know if this is the direction you are meant to take.

If you want to develop more faith, start paying attention to what I call "clues from the universe." When you are considering a course of action, things will start to show up that let you know if this is the direction you are meant to take. Clues showed up for me to direct me toward my speaking career. When I was building my sales organization and taking care of Kate, I kept getting clues. People would walk up to me and ask me to speak somewhere, or people would stop me and say, "I love the way you think; would you be my coach?" Somebody stopped me and asked, "Do you have a book out?" This kind of "prodding" just kept happening. I wondered if I had time for a speaking venture, but then my inner Small Voice got so loud and the clues got so big, that I knew this was my real direction. Those clues have blossomed into my true assignment. I was meant to share these principles with you. Thank you for picking up this book. As you read and learn, you allow me to be in my assignment.

I will share with you a beautiful story about life and its clues. One day when my daughter Katie was four years old, I heard her calling from the bedroom, "Mommy, MOMMY!" I peeked around the corner to see her lying prone on my bed, her feet in the air and her head in her hands, staring ahead. I laughed to myself, wondering what was inside that inquisitive mind of hers now.

"Mommy, what do God's angels look like?"

As I mentally tried to prepare an answer that would have some meaning for her, she chimed in, "I want to go and see them."

"We can't," I automatically responded, forgoing my thoughtful answer.

"But Mommy, I want to go and see an angel, please," she pleaded.

"Sweet Pea, the angels are always here with us. We can't always see them, but they're here."

"But we can see them sometimes, right?"

"Sure we can," I answered, feeling like I was getting into a little hot water.

"Okay, Mommy, please show me the next time you see an angel."

She smiled with delight as she jumped off the bed and headed for her next problem to be solved. I sat down on my bed and thought about what I had said. I could hope that she would just forget the inquiry, and I would be off the hook—but I knew Katie, and that didn't seem likely.

As the world would have it, the very next day I filled Katie's request and met an angel. She came upon me quite by surprise. Actually, this angel was lost and looking for the bus stop. I was at Katie's school for a special holiday program, when an older woman appeared from nowhere, trying to take a shortcut behind the school to a nearby bus bench. I knew the route she wanted to take was impassable and thought about the best directions to give. It was a long walk to the bus, and it was noon in Florida—not the best combination.

I saw our chance meeting that day as a gift from heaven.

I glanced at my watch. The school program was starting any minute. I offered the lady a quick lift down the street and she happily accepted. You never know what kind of gifts will be sent your way. My passenger was more than delightful. A well-educated, retired physician from the Boston area, she filled my car with the sweet sound of an amazing life lived and adventures yet to be dared. My intrigue outweighed my concern for the school program; after all, they always started late.

I soon discovered that her final destination was close by and I persuaded her to let me take her there, only a few minutes away by car. Hearing about her activities and her plans captivated me. She offered not only her own rich presence, but also seemed to draw forth my own inner radiance. Although I was providing the ride, I felt that I was getting the favor. Before we parted, I formally introduced myself and gave her my home phone number. I expressed a sincere wish that we could get together for coffee, and we said our goodbyes.

It was a sweet exchange and left me feeling very good that day. She had a unique and endearing way about her. Although she was the truly great storyteller, her questions and interests in me and my stories were genuine and enthusiastic. She had touched upon a cherished dream of mine without knowing it. She spoke of writing, of me telling my story and writing my book. Unbeknown to her, I was a closet author, just waiting to get started. She lit a spark. I saw our chance meeting that day as a gift from heaven. Who was this wonderful woman who had such an obvious lust for life? I suspected that would be the last I saw of Brenda O. Frankel.

To my great pleasure, I received a phone call from Ms. Frankel just two days later. As it turned out, she was in need of an apartment, and the card that I had given her was one of my business cards. I was, at that time, a realtor who dealt with apartments. This was synchronicity. And so our acquaintance continued for several days to follow, as we looked for apartments and explored the area. I stood in wonder as I watched this woman with every new person we encountered. She would swiftly see something wonderful about everyone and point it out in a subtle manner for all to see. Every person whom we met walked away with a smile. How incredible! To live in a world where you see the good part in everyone first. And then in between our real estate appointments, she would share stories of books that she had read, or had written, or was planning to write.

Brenda Frankel, in a very short time, impacted my life. She inspired me and served as a model for what I want to be. I want to be in that world where I see the good in everyone first, where I constantly look to educate and improve myself, and continue forever to live my life fully.

As for a description of angels, as far as I can tell, they stand about five feet, four inches tall, wear casual clothes, and have short, light-brown **Examine your life for angels.** hair. They wear glasses and have a firm handshake, a beautiful smile, and a magical spark in their eyes. They have a sincere interest in everyone around them, and a concern that is heartfelt. They are eighty years old and they wear sneakers. As for your request, my dear Kate, not only can I tell you what angels look like, I can tell you who they are. They are those people who are placed in our presence to make our lives better, to keep us safer, and to direct us to the knowledge that we need. Mostly, they are those who help to keep us on purpose, who open our hearts, and who have an unmistakable effect on our lives.

Examine your life for angels. Look at the people around you, those close to you, or mere acquaintances, or even those who have briefly passed through your life. Have you encountered any angels? Have you experienced any events that directed you toward your true purpose? Begin to look for clues that a higher order exists. I am going to ask you now to trust—to trust that what I tell you is the truth because I know it is. I want you also to trust yourself and to trust what truths your inner knowing provides for you.

Now I want to pass on to you some of the most profound advice that anyone, anywhere, has ever given, written by Mother Teresa.

> *People are often unreasonable, illogical and self-centered.*
>
> *Forgive them anyway.*
>
> *If you are kind, people may accuse you of selfish, ulterior motives.*
>
> *Be kind anyway.*
>
> *If you are successful, you will win some false friends and some true enemies.*
>
> *Succeed anyway.*

If you are honest and frank, people may cheat you.

Be honest and frank anyway.

If you find serenity and happiness, they may be jealous.

Be happy anyway.

The good you do today, people will often forget tomorrow.

But do good anyway.

Give the world the best you have and it may never be enough.

But give the world the best you have anyway.

You see, in the final analysis, it is between you and God.

It was never between you and them, anyway.

Without a doubt, my favorite part of the G.A.M.E.S. formula is the magic of surrender. We have been through **Gratitude** and maintaining the consciousness of gratitude. We have explored **Acknowledge,** acknowledging what you are reclaiming, and using the law of "As If." We've covered how and why to **Meditate** and understand silence. We've discussed how to **Energize,** doing those things we need for our physical being, including nurturing the loving part of our being. The glue that holds all else together is **Surrender,** for to surrender is to give faith a chance.

Exercise 10:
Time to Finalize

Now is the time to finish your reclamation statements. Make sure that they all work within the formula: positive, present-day ownership statements that have an emotional charge for you. As you build the culture of you, keep in mind the quote by Mother Teresa, and remember that these statements are uniquely about and for you, in relationship to your God and your universe.

Chapter 11:
Now What?

Y ou have finished building your reclamation statements. Now it is time to put them to work. At this exciting juncture, you will take everything you have learned about being an active participant in building a pathway to your personal prosperity and you will activate it! We have spent a lot of time changing your conscious mind by uncovering how you really think, focusing on what is truly important to you, and understanding the voice under the voice. We are now going to change the nonconscious part of your thinking as well as the conscious part. We know that thoughts and feelings play a major part in what and how we create. Remember, the nonconscious part of our mind creates at a ratio of six to one.

The magic begins now, as you record your reclamation statements on an audiotape in your own voice. When you listen to something in your own voice, it will address the nonconscious part of your thinking and begin to affect real change. Your personal motivator and partner in creativity is your Reclamation Tape. Once the tape is recorded, all you have to do is listen to it for twenty minutes at the beginning of every day. As your conscious and nonconscious thoughts change effortlessly, you will attract and create those things you truly desire, and see real changes in your life. I want to congratulate you on making the decision to reclaim your life.

Exercise 11:
Your Personal Motivator and Partner in Creativity

PART 1: Record

Record your tape of reclamation statements. Repeat the statements over and over again, until you have recorded at least twenty minutes or longer.

PART 2: Listen

Listen to your tape at the beginning of every day for at least twenty minutes.

Chapter 12:
You Already Have What You Need To Get What You Want

I want you to know something very significant about yourself. The fact that you expended the time and energy to read this book plucks you out of the stream of the ordinary. You have now situated yourself on the bank of possibility. The current of time can no longer sweep you toward a future of heedless thoughts, limited attitudes, and unfulfilled dreams. You have a different perspective now, perched in a spot from which you can survey your life, where you came from, and where you want to go. You know now that you can choose not to be carried passively through the rest of your life, at the mercy of every obstacle in your path. You can determine the kind of future you will have, and you have already taken the first steps. You have done some amazing work, taking the time to be with you, invest in yourself, get inside, and uncover the real you. I am so proud of you for exploring these ideas and staying committed to yourself. I deeply respect the work you have already done.

There is a phrase in the preceding paragraph that represents the crux of my message to you. That phrase is "uncover the real you." I want you to remember always that when you do the work of reclamation, you are indeed reclaiming, that is, reasserting, your ownership of that which was already within you. You came into this world with a purpose and with a ready-made scaffold to build your life on that purpose. Never doubt that. When the work of reclamation seems too difficult, be comforted and inspired by the fact that everything you need is already within you.

You do not have to allow others to hold you back.

I have some bits of advice that I want to share with you as you begin this new venture, this new stage of your life. First, here is something to watch for as you progress. We all have loved ones, people with whom we live in close proximity, or those whose lives intertwine with ours. It is difficult and awkward when these people don't grow and change as we do. Don't expect to change others. If friction arises when you make beneficial changes in your life, you can ask others to acknowledge your right to change, and to let you progress in your own life, even if they don't want to come with you. You do not have to allow others to hold you back.

Now I have some advisory comments about risk-taking. What exactly is risk? The definition of risk is the chance of injury, damage, or loss. When we attempt something, and the results are not what we wanted, we think of this as a failure. This concept of failure signifies injury and loss to our ego, our self-esteem, and thus, what keeps us from risking is really the fear of failing. I would like to offer you a different way of thinking about risk and failure right now. I want to quote the last two lines of a poem written by Alfred, Lord Tennyson in the 1800s: "'Tis better to have loved and lost than never to have loved at all." In these lines, he has sent us a message that is all too often ignored by those who live in fear of failing. He tells us to go into life as if failure were not even a consideration, and to ignore our fears as we move forward. I think these words are among the most memorable and most quoted in all of literature, but how many people actually heed the words?

Consider this concept: there is no such thing as failure. Failure is a judgment that we humans place on any given act. It is a conversation that we have in our head. We have the option of replacing self-recrimination with words such as this: "I cannot fail; I can only produce an alternative outcome." Rumi says, "Out there beyond right and wrong-doing, there is a field. Come join me there." We can think beyond the narrow confines of wrong and right outcomes.

In my opinion, it is better to jump in and experience life than to stand on the sidelines, fearing that something might go wrong. We can decide that any result is an indication that we are taking action toward our goal, even

Our very nature is to seek advancement.

when it is not the ideal result. I once heard a delightful retort that Thomas Edison made to a reporter, who had asked him how it felt to have failed 25,000 times in his effort to invent the battery. His response was "I haven't failed. Today, I know 25,000 ways not to make a battery."

Let me give you another example. When we were infants, before we were subjected to our own judgments, we wanted to learn to crawl, and then to walk. What if we had sat back and said, "I am not going to learn to walk because I might fall." There was always the risk of falling, and undoubtedly, we did fall a number of times. But eventually, we stood up and started walking. Our basic nature wouldn't let us remain satisfied with crawling. I suggest to you that our very nature is to seek advancement, and it is my belief that we should all proceed through our life doing just that. It is far better to have acted and produced some sort of outcome, and one that we could possibly grow from, than to sit back and live in fear.

Only those who risk are free.

I want you to know in your heart that you have never failed at anything, and you never will. Failure is just an artificial judgment that you have made in your own mind; it is mistakes and errors that keep us moving forward, and it is those same mistakes and errors that are the very foundation of real growth. You see, the greatest risk of all is to risk nothing, because to live this way is to chain yourself to mediocrity and limitation. Only those who risk are free. The prizes of greater wisdom and inner strength always go to those who take, in one way or another, the risk. In the words of Helen Keller, "Life is either a daring adventure—or nothing."

I keep with me, on the mantel at home, a piece of coal. I also take it with me when I travel to speaking events. I use it as a reminder, first of where I came from, and second of where we can all go. I grew up in a small coal-mining town in Pennsylvania. Do you know what can happen to a lump of coal? Under the right circumstances, it can become a diamond. How does this happen? Through pressure, heat, and time. In other words, a piece of coal is a diamond without the pressure.

We are all like diamonds. We come into being with unseen, magnificent potential, and then pressure, "heat," and time forge us, transforming us to expose the treasure hidden within. The rough diamond, as it comes from the mine, must undergo cutting and polishing to bring forth its brilliance. And so it is with us. It takes care, effort, and judgment to uncover our splendor. We talked about personal prosperity, taking all the parts of our lives and consciously creating every "facet." We must polish every facet of our lives to shine as we were meant to. Say to yourself, "My life is a brilliant diamond."

As you are cutting and polishing the facets of your life, remember the ideas you have learned in this book. The Law of Creative Thought tells you that thoughts are things. What you think about, whether positive or negative, creates your own personal circumstances in life. You are designing your own destiny right now; make sure you are doing so consciously, with deliberate direction. Eliminate counterproductive life scripts and replace them with conscious, active choices to achieve your goals. Avoid default decisions. Acknowledge the Law of Responsibility—accept personal responsibility for your situation and drive your own decision-making machinery.

Use the Law of Focus on what you want, and allow your energies to create it. Remember, you don't have to know how your dreams will be fulfilled. You need only know exactly **Attitude is everything.** what it is that you want. Once you establish clarity of intent, the Law of Attraction will bring to you the people and events that allow you to achieve your goals. You can reclaim the parts of yourself and your life that you have disowned through improper scripting. Use the Law of "As If" to get what you want by assuming the mindset that what you want already exists for you. What is going to keep you in action? Not limiting thinking. You can have the magic and the miracles that life offers if you exercise magical thinking and believe in miracles. Attitude is everything. You can have your desires fulfilled. Just maintain the belief that it will happen.

If we believe these principles, harness them, and put them to work, we can create the things we want. I drew upon many sources over the years as my inspiration for the G.A.M.E.S. formula. You can use my formula as your pathway to personal action, taking the steps that will make your life work for you. Here is a brief reminder of what your daily G.A.M.E.S. steps are: Be in **Gratitude,** be grateful for every breath. **Acknowledge** what, and whom, you are reclaiming. **Meditate** and listen to the song of your own heart. **Energize** by eating right, exercising, and nourishing the whole you, including that part of you that gives and seeks love. And **Surrender.** Faith, detachment, and uncertainty equate to mystery and magic.

It is a fact that there are opportunities everywhere.

It has been said that many people read good books, but do not get much good out of them. If you merely discover these secrets, but you don't use them, they will be as meaningless as if you never found them at all. Don't lock them away in the closets of your mind. The Laws of Life and the G.A.M.E.S. formula are realistic, practical ideas at your disposal. Activate them. Put them to work for you now and for as long as you live.

It is for this purpose that I created the Reclamation Tape. Although your ideal goal is listening for twenty minutes, even five minutes a day will be helpful. Try it and observe the results in your daily life. I promise you won't regret the time it takes to do so.

Don't ever let naysayers persuade you that opportunities to fulfill your dreams are lacking. It is a fact that there are opportunities everywhere. I want to illustrate this point with a story about my beloved Dave. He grew up in Africa. When he was

It is just the beginning for you.

five years old, he used to stand next to the Zambezi River at Victoria Falls and try to catch bubbles in a bucket. The bubbles just kept coming, no matter how many he caught in his bucket. As he grew up, he equated those bubbles with opportunity. You see, we have never-ending opportunities. We just don't believe that we have them. So I want you to see the river, and I want you to see the bubbles and know with certainty that opportunities are as ceaseless as those bubbles. Just be open to them and keep that belief.

This may look like the end of my book, but it is just the beginning for you. My message is already spilling into your thought patterns and the way you function. At the end of this chapter, there is a revised contract with yourself to read, sign, and date. It is similar to the contract you signed earlier, but it reinforces your determination to hold the course you have set. I have provided in Appendix A a summary of the Laws of Life for quick reference. Appendix B is a set of forty encouraging reminders to help keep the concepts you have learned circulating through your mind. Read one of these every day, and then, when you have gone through the whole list, start over again, and continue for as long as you need to. Remember that life is a process. Allow yours to unfold with all the glory, the magic, the mystery, and the brilliance it was meant to have.

I want to assure you that I'm behind you. I really believe in YOU. Your life is a brilliant diamond. It is one of my cherished dreams that you will walk the path of adventure you were meant to choose. Thus, each day, as I listen to my own Reclamation Tape and acknowledge my own goals, I will also be acknowledging your goals. Together we can do it. Dare to make this life remarkable!

To solidify your self-commitment to use the Laws of Life and participate daily in G.A.M.E.S., please read, sign, and date the following contract with yourself. In so doing, you will ensure the adventures you were born to have.

Please read, sign, and date:

I, _____ , pledge to stay on the path to my own personal truth. I commit myself to my growth. I commit to applying the Laws of Life and the G.A.M.E.S. formula daily, to direct the course of my future. I will do the work I need to do.

_____

Signature

_____

Date

Appendix A:
The Laws of Life

1. The Law of Creative Thought

Thoughts are things. Your conscious—and most importantly, your nonconscious—thoughts are constantly creating both the material and nonmaterial things in your life, whether you are aware of it or not.

2. The Law of Focus

What you consciously and consistently focus upon shows up for you. You must first make a decision as to what you want to create or accomplish, and then focus your thoughts and energies on it. Just as physically focusing your eyes can bring something into view, mentally focusing your thoughts can bring what you want into your life.

3. The Law of Responsibility

You are responsible for you. Regardless of the past, regardless of what others may want for you, you are accountable for your life, your actions, your reactions, and those things that you bring into creation.

4. The Law of Attraction

Whether you know it or not, you are always attracting into your life people and situations. When you become clear about your goals, when you develop clarity of intent and hold that intention, you start to draw what you want toward you.

5. The Law of "As If"

If you assume the feeling of fulfillment of a desire "as if" you already possess it, then life conspires to grant you actual fulfillment. You must imagine the thoughts and feelings of the goal fulfilled, with all the sensory vividness of reality. See it in your mind, feel it in your heart, know that it has already come true. The scope of this law is the most expansive, because it incorporates the principles of the other four laws.

Appendix B:
Encouraging Reminders

F ollowing are forty remarks meant to support, encourage, inspire, and remind you of the timeless principles you have learned. Read one each day for forty days. Why forty? The symbolism of the number "forty" resonates through the ages in association with human development. Approximately forty days from conception, the embryo achieves recognizable human form, and at roughly forty weeks, birth occurs. Beginning with our primitive ancestors, this number was comprehended in terms of gestation and incubation.

References to a period of forty days or forty years occur in scriptures from around the world, including those of Christianity, Judaism, Islam, and Buddhism. This interval universally signifies a course of probation, meaning a time of critical examination and evaluation, or a time of testing and trial. In many cases, the period represented by the number forty involves an ascent from one level to the next highest, a metamorphosis or a cataclysmic change and new creation. Examples include Noah's flood of forty days and forty nights, the wandering of the Israelites for forty years, and the temptation of Jesus for forty days. The ancient Greeks and Romans associated the age of forty years with maturity and responsibility. Muhammad began his ministry at the age of forty. Buddha sat under the bodhi tree for approximately forty days during the bliss of his enlightenment. Thus, in the age-old tradition of humankind, I would like for you to use the next forty-day period of your life as a time of preparation, grace, and renewal.

Day 1

Now that you've finished reading the book, it's up to you to use your new tools and create the amazing life you were born to live. Remember to take those few minutes as you start your day to listen to your Reclamation Tape. It just takes twenty minutes a day. You can do it! Engage the PPT Factor—"push play today."

Day 2

You were born to live a life filled with wonder and magnificence, because that is who you are. Reclaiming your power, your motivation, your joy, your sense of self . . . your life of infinite possibility . . . is as easy as remembering to press the "play" button. Remember to take those precious twenty minutes at the beginning of your day today, as time well spent with YOU. Remember the PPT Factor and "push play today."

PS—oops! If you're reading this in the afternoon or evening, and you didn't listen to your tape this morning . . . you can do it NOW!

Day 3

Gratitude is the rudder that keeps our lives on course. Start each day by remembering ten things for which you are grateful, ten simple things that rock your world, stir your heart, and awaken your aliveness . . . starting with YOU! And remember to include the PPT Factor: "push play today" and reclaim your life!

Day 4

The voice of greatness whispers within. Are you listening? Can you hear it? The more you listen to your Reclamation Tape, the louder that guiding voice of greatness becomes.

Remember the PPT Factor: "push play today" and summon forth the greatness that you are!

Day 5

What you choose to focus on today, you are creating in your world. You have the ability to live your dreams and make your goals reality. All it takes is making the choice to focus the power of your intention. The Reclamation Tape is one of your most powerful tools, so please, remember to engage the PPT Factor and "push play today."

Day 6

By giving daily attention to creating your own inner culture and renewing your decision to live your life, you change the future. Everything is possible with the PPT Factor . . . remember to make time to "push play today."

Day 7

By cultivating and feeding your garden of conscious thought daily, you can and will reap a bountiful harvest of dreams fulfilled. It's as simple as engaging the PPT Factor! "Push play today" and watch the magic happen.

Day 8

Every thought has creative potential and we have the power to choose which thoughts we enliven with our attention. Losers visualize the penalties of losing. Winners visualize the rewards of success. The choice is yours. With the PPT Factor, you can "push play today" and enliven the winner that you truly are.

Day 9

Here's your daily reminder. Everything depends on your attitude toward yourself. That which you cannot acknowledge as true of yourself can never be fully realized or embodied. Remember to plug in the PPT Factor. "Push play today" and give yourself a tailor-made attitude adjustment . . . a gift of love from you to you.

Day 10

Creating the life you were born to live requires faith and trust . . . faith in yourself and faith in your Universe. The PPT Factor offers a powerful way to ignite your faith and trust. Just "push play today" and watch that fire burn.

Day 11

Action steps are among the most potent secrets to success. Be they small or great, each one takes you further along the path of fulfillment. The PPT Factor action step, taken daily, insignificant as it may seem, yields BIG results. Just "push play today." It's as simple as that!

Day 12

Remember . . . to live your vision you must acknowledge the thoughts and feelings of the desire or wish
fulfilled, until you have all the sensory vividness of
its reality. You must imagine that you are already
experiencing that which you desire. The PPT Factor
is your most potent ally in enlivening your imagination. "Push play today" and feel the difference.

Day 13

Love is the essence of life. Love is as essential as food and water. Without it, we cannot survive. Remember to love yourself today, be kind to yourself today, treasure yourself today. By engaging the PPT Factor, you take another step toward living the Love you are. "Push play today" and open your heart to the magic of life.

Day 14

Through mastering your inner dialogue, you can transform your reality and create the things you want in your life. The PPT Factor is the key to re-scripting your life. "Push play today" to turn up the volume on your inner voice of possibility.

Day 15

By changing your thoughts and beliefs, you can change any aspect of your life and engage the dynamic Law of Attraction. Remember the PPT Factor: "Push play today" to amplify your innate magnetism.

Day 16

All limiting beliefs, feelings, and emotional states can instantaneously expand today to align with prosperity, ease, and success. Just put the PPT Factor to work for you. "Push play today" and turn your limitless nature into greatness.

Day 17

What you think about expands. By feeding your mind positive, uplifting thoughts and images, you make yourself available to miracles every day. Your Reclamation Tape is the key that unlocks those miracles. Remember to partake of the PPT Factor today. "Push play today" and nourish your life.

Day 18

A garden flourishes most when tended, cultivated, and fertilized; if left to itself, all too soon it is over-taken by weeds. Cultivate the garden of your own mind with the PPT Factor. "Push play today" and watch your intentions flourish and bloom in unexpected and wonderful ways.

Day 19

The universe in which we live is strangely and wonderfully accommodating. Whatever our point of view, we will find ourselves attracting evidence of its validity. You can change your reality by shifting your perspective. The PPT Factor is a key. "Push play today" and shift your world.

Day 20

The more you praise and celebrate your life, the more there is in life to celebrate. Take time each day to be in gratitude for everything and everyone. The PPT Factor is your key to success beyond your imagining. "Push play today" . . . and every day . . . and watch the wondrous miracle that is your life unfold in ease and joy.

Day 21

Spending time with you is essential for self-nurturing. Nature has a way of quicting our thoughts. Stroll on the beach, walk in the park, hike in the woods, watch a sunrise or sunset. Your silent spot is a magical way to uncover you. Utilize the PPT Factor as another way to spend time with you today. Just "push play today" and let the unfolding begin.

Day 22

The way we think about ourselves, about others, about our surroundings, and our passions, runs our lives. Our thoughts and our attitudes literally make our lives take form. Use the PPT Factor, "push play today," and take conscious action to form your life in the way you want.

Day 23

Life is here to be completely enjoyed and fully lived. The thin line between an ordinary and extraordinary life has now been exposed for you. Leading the charge to reclaim your life is you. This difference-making discovery is now in your hands. Just utilize the PPT Factor, "push play today," and put all you have learned into action.

Day 24

One of the mightiest Laws of Life is that thoughts are things. Things which lay out, construct, and dictate your life. This is called creative thought. When you reengineer your thoughts, you can redesign your life. Use your creative thinking and redesign those things that you want changed. Use the PPT Factor: "push play today," and effortlessly allow your thoughts to consciously become part of who you really are.

Day 25

Do you remember how you felt at eighteen? The dizzying, dynamic possibilities of the world ahead were only limited by the scope of your imagination. Success and personal freedom may have been out of focus since then, but they are still not out of reach. At this pivotal juncture of your life's journey, settling for less is not an option. Use the PPT Factor, and "push play today" to reclaim your potential and reopen the inner power that you have always had.

Day 26

The richness of your life is in direct proportion to your willingness to be in your own discovery. This means it takes work. Life is work. Your life is your responsibility. You are accountable for your life's journey. Use the PPT Factor: "push play today," as your personal motivator and partner in creativity, as you make your life work for you.

Day 27

There is something very potent about making a decision. When you make a decision consciously and purposefully, you put energetic forces into play. The by-product of a real decision is determination, a firm conviction and attitude that can abolish self-doubt. By using the PPT Factor, "push play today," and you can cement those conscious decisions into place.

Day 28

As you look at statements to add to your Reclamation Tape, use the wisdom of the O.W.L. formula to examine new goals and ideas.

O—Obedience—be true to yourself

W—Willingness—to do what it takes

L—Listening—to your own thoughts

The PPT Factor, "push play today," will help those goals and ideas come to life.

Day 29

Here is a bright truth for you to carry always in your heart: even though sorrow plays a role in every life, our birthright is prosperity and abundance and happiness and joy.

Use this certainty as your foundation for living. And with the PPT Factor, "push play today," you can build your life in the most remarkable way.

Day 30

You do not need to know how something is going to happen. You need only to develop real clarity of intent, and hold the intention. You can then start to draw people and situations into your life to fulfill that intention. The PPT Factor, "push play today," is a powerful way to keep your intention on track.

Day 31

Self-renewal is not only possible, but also desirable and healthy. Renewal benefits and transforms us. You can rejuvenate that fresh, dazzling sense of possibility to revive old dreams and reclaim parts of yourself. The PPT Factor, "push play today," will give you that edge to constantly renew your mind. Through this renewal you can reclaim your power, your motivation, your joy, your sense of self, and your life.

Day 32

The great secret to conscious creation is controlled imagination and well-sustained attention, firmly and repeatedly placed on that which you desire. Distraction is the enemy to this action. Your Reclamation Tape has been engineered to keep you out of distraction. Use the PPT Factor, "push play today," and let one of life's great secrets work for you.

Day 33

Your trigger switch statements are personal messages of comfort or confirmations of faith. Keep your trigger switch mentally handy to replace anything negative that may occur. Memorizing a few trigger switches may neutralize unwelcome situations. When you find yourself having feelings that don't suit you, just hit the switch in your mind. Use the PPT factor, "push play today," to instill all of your statements effortlessly.

Day 34

You can influence your health and your body by the choices you make. The thoughts, attitudes, and intentions you choose affect your physical well-being; in turn, the way you treat your body influences your mental and emotional state. The PPT Factor, "push play today," can be a powerful ally in incorporating basic rules of good health into your lifestyle.

Day 35

A restful mind and a rested body generate creativity and renewal. Real recovery time promotes vitality and energy. Recovery time means having time away, from whatever you are doing, to rejuvenate. Go to a movie, have a massage, read a book, play with your children, take a walk or a power nap. You can use the PPT Factor, "push play today," as another way to just be with you.

Day 36

Love buffers, tempers, and actually transforms biology. It motivates you to do great things. It is a life-sustaining force. The next time you have a choice between a loving or non-loving thought or action, choose the loving one. With the PPT Factor, "push play today," you can use your statements to be always conscious of your loving, caring, and nurturing activities.

Day 37

Napoleon Hill says that when faith blends with thought, the subconscious mind then translates it to its spiritual equivalent, and transmits it to infinite intelligence. He also states that those thoughts that have been given feeling, mixed with faith, begin immediately to translate into their physical counterpart. Listen to your Reclamation Tape, use the PPT Factor, and "push play today," having all the faith and the knowing that your life's miracles are unfolding for you.

Day 38

Faith requires us to relinquish control. Faith requires that we trust. Most of us have inner dreams that we can uncover if we have the courage to take a look, spend time with ourselves, and then to accept what we have discovered. Then we must have the faith to act on what we have discovered. The PPT Factor, "push play today," can be your master guide as you move forward on your own path to personal discovery.

Day 39

Faith removes limitations. Faith is the greatest transforming power of all of life. It brings in its wake the divine inheritances of health, happiness, joy, and a more abundant life. The PPT Factor, "push play today," can be an amazing force in helping you to cultivate your faith.

Day 40

We are at the fortieth day. You have been utilizing your powerful creative tool, your Reclamation Tape. I know things have been shifting in your world. Bear in mind that this is not the end, but truly the beginning. Use this tool every day. Make it part of what you do. Ask yourself, "Did I engage the PPT Factor, 'push play today'?" Change it when you need to. Allow your life to unfold into its passion and purpose.

It is one of my cherished dreams that you will walk the path of adventure you were meant to choose. Thus, each day as I listen to my own Reclamation Tape, acknowledging my own dreams, I will also be acknowledging yours. Together we can do it.

About the Author

Kandee G is a successful entrepreneur and businesswoman whose "rags to riches" story is an inspiration to many. She is a sales coach, life skills coach, speaker, author, and personal motivator. A recognized leader in the motivational speaking industry, Kandee G teaches universal, timeless principles and real-time action steps based on her own twenty-five-year path of study. By revealing the secrets to true success, happiness, and personal prosperity, she shows others how to master their own lives.

The mission of Kandee G Enterprises, Inc. is to make a difference in people's lives. Kandee G and her G Force team provide clients with the tools to discover their own remarkable lives. Join the whole team at an upcoming event so that you can learn how to "reclaim your remarkable life."

For information on events with Kandee G or available products and services, please contact: www.kandeeg.com or call 1-888-kandeeg (526-3334)

Kandee G has been gifted with the ability to help people change their lives.

—Les Brown

Kandee G is also available to customize programs for your corporation, group, or organization.

Contact the Author

If this book makes a difference in your life, we would deeply appreciate your letting us know. Please e-mail your stories to kandeeg@kandeeg.com or call 1-888-kandeeg (526-3334).